Cambridge Elements

Elements in Business Strategy
edited by
J.-C. Spender
Rutgers Business Schc

T0286094

AUSTRIAN PERSPECTIVES ON ENTREPRENEURSHIP, STRATEGY, AND ORGANIZATION

Nicolai J. Foss
Bocconi University

Peter G. Klein
Baylor University

Matthew McCaffrey
University of Manchester

CAMBRIDGE
UNIVERSITY PRESS

CAMBRIDGE
UNIVERSITY PRESS

University Printing House, Cambridge CB2 8BS, United Kingdom

One Liberty Plaza, 20th Floor, New York, NY 10006, USA

477 Williamstown Road, Port Melbourne, VIC 3207, Australia

314–321, 3rd Floor, Plot 3, Splendor Forum, Jasola District Center, New Delhi – 110025, India

79 Anson Road, #06–04/06, Singapore 079906

Cambridge University Press is part of the University of Cambridge.

It furthers the University's mission by disseminating knowledge in the pursuit of education, learning, and research at the highest international levels of excellence.

www.cambridge.org
Information on this title: www.cambridge.org/9781108745802
DOI: 10.1017/9781108777742

First published 2019

A catalogue record for this publication is available from the British Library.

ISBN 978-1-108-74580-2 Paperback
ISSN 2515-0693 (online)
ISSN 2515-0685 (print)

Austrian Perspectives on Entrepreneurship, Strategy, and Organization

Elements in Business Strategy

DOI: 10.1017/9781108777742
First published online: August 2019

Nicolai J. Foss
Bocconi University

Peter G. Klein
Baylor University

Matthew McCaffrey
University of Manchester

Author for correspondence: Nicolai J. Foss, nicolai.foss@unibocconi.it

Abstract: The "Austrian" tradition is well-known for its definitive contributions to economics in the twentieth century. However, Austrian economics also offers an exciting research agenda outside the traditional boundaries of economics, especially in the management disciplines. This Element examines how Austrian ideas play a key role in expanding our understanding of fields like entrepreneurship, strategy, and organization. It focuses especially on the vital role that entrepreneurs play in guiding economic progress by shaping firms and their strategic behavior. In doing so, it explains a wide range of contributions Austrian economics makes to our understanding of key problems in management, while also highlighting many directions for future work in this inspiring tradition.

ISBNs: 9781108745802 (PB), 9781108777742 (OC)
ISSNs: 2515-0693 (online), 2515-0685 (print)

Contents

Preface

Much of current management thinking owes a great debt to Austrian economics. To be sure, this influence is largely indirect. But the person who is arguably still the dominant thought-leader in management studies, the Austrian-American Peter Drucker, was well-versed in Austrian economics. In fact, as a young man he met and interacted with key Austrian economists, notably Ludwig von Mises, Joseph Schumpeter, and Friedrich Hayek. Little research exists on the Austrian roots of Drucker's thinking, but it is a plausible hypothesis that many of his key ideas – such as his emphasis on decentralization in business firms, the role of knowledge workers, importance of innovation as the only lasting source of competitive advantage, and skepticism about macro thinking – reflect his exposure to the Austrian tradition.[1]

In a similar way, we believe there is huge unexploited potential for bringing Austrian economic ideas into management thought. More generally, we believe that in many important ways Austrian economists speak a language closer to the one spoken by management scholars than to the language of mainstream economics. This book is therefore written in the belief that Austrian economics still has much to offer to management studies. Our dominant Austrian influence is Ludwig von Mises. This may at first seem strange, as F.A. Hayek's ideas have often been drawn upon in management studies, while Mises remains a less appreciated figure. And yet, Mises' thinking on the entrepreneur and the market process is in many ways different from Hayek's and is perhaps of even greater relevance to management research. We therefore dedicate this book to the memory of two very different, but both towering (in their respective domains) individuals, Ludwig von Mises and Peter Drucker.

We are grateful to JC Spender for suggesting the idea for this Element.

1 Introduction

The Uniqueness of the Austrian School

The "Austrian" school of economics, named for its nineteenth-century origins in Vienna, is well-known for its contributions to economics over the past century-and-a-half. To take only a few examples, Austrian economists pioneered the economic critique of socialism and the analysis of the entrepreneurial market economy; their ideas were used to predict and to explain both the Great Depression and the Great Recession; and Austrian scholars have also launched radical and unique criticisms of organizations and policies, including monetary and banking institutions. Yet while the methods, concepts, and theories of the

---

[1] The exception is Kiessling and Richey (2004).

Austrians have mainly been applied in their home discipline of economics, they are also becoming more widespread in management studies. This is especially true in the disciplines of entrepreneurship, strategy, and organization studies.

In general, many Austrian school ideas are not only compatible with, but also, we shall argue, provide superior foundations for contemporary management studies. However, many management scholars, practitioners, and educators have little knowledge of Austrian economics or know it only through its association with libertarian political philosophy. Austrian economic ideas are still not taught in many university and business school programs. Furthermore, over the long history of the school some of its ideas have been absorbed into the economic mainstream and are no longer treated as distinct contributions.[2] Nevertheless, many of its core ideas have not, and it is those on which we focus in this section. We specifically have in mind Austrian ideas about the subjectivity of decision-making, dispersed knowledge, heterogeneity of capital, importance of uncertainty and entrepreneurial decision-making, and the need to provide a realistic, causally-informed understanding of economic processes. Thus, one overall purpose of this Element is to argue broadly for the usefulness of Austrian economics in informing and furthering management research. An indispensable part of this, of course, is providing introductions to those Austrian ideas with the potential to do so.

The Relevance of Austrian Economics to Management Thought

The many unique emphases of Austrian economics – its focus on realism, causality, value, consumer choice, prices, uncertainty, process, entrepreneurship, heterogeneous capital, and social coordination – make it ideally suited as a foundation for many management disciplines. For instance, each of the three major examples mentioned in the previous section is based on a unique understanding of the role of entrepreneurs in society: the performance of socialist economies depends on their ability – or lack thereof – to draw on the entrepreneurial division of labor; business cycles can only be understood by considering how entrepreneurs behave during booms and busts; the economic implications of alternative banking institutions depend first and foremost on how entrepreneurs create and use them.

If we turn from entrepreneurship to the seemingly very different topic of the internal organization of companies, Austrian economics also has much useful insight to provide. One example has to do with what Austrians call the "division

---

[2] We admire much of so-called mainstream economics and do not reject the use of formal methods in theory and empirics as such. However, we do think that mainstream economics has a number of "blind spots".

of knowledge" (a way to emphasize the point that the division of labor is usually accompanied by a corresponding specialization in terms of knowledge). The first economist to persuasively suggest that the division of knowledge has enormous implications for organization was F. A. Hayek, who specifically argued that the division of knowledge requires decentralization. Utilizing knowledge that is highly relevant for decision-making, but that is also dispersed, fleeting, etc., requires that the decision-maker be given the right to act on that knowledge. Arguably, many companies committed to overly hierarchical decision structures have yet to absorb and understand this basic idea, which was the primary motivation behind the award of the Nobel Prize in Economics to Hayek in 1974.

To take another example, beginning with the school's founder, Carl Menger, Austrians have also often emphasized that many of society's most valued and important institutions are products of partly "blind" social processes.[3] That is, they have not been explicitly designed by anyone, but have nevertheless emerged to serve a useful social purpose. This is true of some of our most fundamental institutions, from money to key aspects of property-rights and the law, etc. Of course, great thought leaders as well as politicians (only weakly overlapping sets) have also intervened in the process of social evolution and partly shaped its course, but much of what is fundamental in the fabric of social life has emerged spontaneously. This idea is also most directly associated with Hayek's research.[4]

Similar points could be made about the "social life" of companies. Companies have cultures, shared values based on often unstated assumptions. Their attempt to make their cultures explicit may lead to the formation of identities that then become part of their mission statements. This can in turn lead to the belief that cultures can be easily manipulated to serve certain company-specific purposes. According to management professor folklore, when the culture craze was at its height in the late 1980s, consultants would get requests from CEOs to "get me a new culture by next week" – and some consultants would in fact claim that they could do this. Of course, anyone with a basic knowledge of how deep-seated and fundamental culture is will be highly skeptical of such claims. Rightly so, as Hayek's work suggests that culture is hard to change precisely because it emerges to serve the changing needs of

---

[3] This theme originated during the "Scottish Enlightenment" through thinkers such as David Hume, Adam Ferguson, and, of course, Adam Smith.

[4] Although Hayek received the Nobel Prize in 1974, he had effectively stopped writing about technical economics several decades earlier. After World War II, most of his work was dedicated to refining his views on classical liberalism and embedding them into an ambitious and sweeping theory of cultural evolution.

people dealing with specific challenges, but also gets internalized in the form of tacit and typically rigid rules of behavior. Thus, in many ways Austrian economics provides a more realistic understanding of the challenges of changing what is colloquially called "corporate DNA," that is, the basic assumptions, beliefs, etc. that characterize the organization.

As a final illustration of the relevance of Austrian economics, consider Corporate Social Responsibility (CSR), currently a highly fashionable trend in management thinking and in managerial practice. Obviously, CSR reflects very much the *Zeitgeist*, specifically, ideas about the overriding importance of sustainability in terms of husbanding the planet's resources, particular ethical positions about business practices, and the claim that people should have some power over the broader social forces that influence them. Thus, CSR puts together "green" concerns, business ethics, and an extended notion of "democracy." While much of this may sound laudable and appealing, Austrian economics warns that much of CSR thinking may rest on shallow foundations.

The fundamental point is that if companies are to make rational decisions concerning CSR actions, they need a way to compare different actions; that is, as Mises (1920) pointed out almost 100 years ago, a common metric is required. His specific argument was directed against the claims of utopian socialists who wanted to abolish markets, centralize resource allocation, and, in classical Marxist fashion, let resources be allocated according to "needs." Mises argued that if markets (in particular, those for capital goods) were eliminated, prices would also cease to exist. Without prices, decision-makers would not know how to make the best use of productive resources because there would be no uniform signals that could be relied on to steer resources to their most valued ends. Profit and loss estimates would be impossible, and the net present values of alternative investment projects could not be calculated. Like utopian socialist planners, many proponents of CSR do not provide a way to assess which CSR investments should be undertaken, how much should be invested, and so on. There is no common metric that can be used for this purpose, or rather, the one that exists, namely, profitability, is often frowned upon. Decision-makers are groping in darkness.[5]

What This Element Does

This Element provides a concise overview of the role of Austrian economics in management studies. We highlight both its current achievements and some

---

[5] An emphasis on CSR, and on giving decision-making authority to a broader set of stakeholders besides the firm's owners, is also in conflict with the Misesian idea that, under uncertainty, entrepreneurship is embodied in ownership and that equity holders have unique advantages in exercising the ownership function (Foss and Klein, 2018).

promising new research directions, some of which we have hinted at already and will discuss further in the following. The Element is intended for management researchers as well as advanced students interested in Austrian economics and what it has to offer the various disciplines within management studies. While we seek to be broad and general, we obviously cannot cover all of management research. Thus, we do not deal with some major disciplines like organizational behavior, operations management, and marketing. While we are confident that Austrian economics also has implications for these areas, our knowledge of them is too meager to offer any particular insights. Thus, our coverage is restricted to the fields of entrepreneurship, strategy, organization, and general management. These are, of course, fields that also inform a number of neighboring areas such as technology management and innovation, international business, and, to some extent, human resource management, all of which are relevant to Austrian economics.

An Overview

We begin in Section 2 with a primer on Austrian economics that surveys key Austrian ideas and briefly links them to important ideas in management thought. These links are then unfolded in the subsequent sections. Section 3 studies the theory of entrepreneurship in detail, explaining some unique Austrian contributions and how they inform contemporary entrepreneurship studies. Section 4 then expands the traditional theory of entrepreneurship in the market to account for alternative forms of entrepreneurial action in social enterprises, political organizations, and among institutions more generally. Section 5 discusses the entrepreneurial foundations of strategy research, and Section 6 explains the entrepreneurial foundations of the theory of the firm. Section 7 concludes with a brief survey of several emerging trends in Austrian management research.

2 What is Austrian Economics?

Origins

The Austrian school was one of three major strands of "neoclassical" economics to emerge from the "marginalist revolution" of the 1870s. The founding of the school is usually dated to 1871, the year economist Carl Menger published his *Principles of Economics*.[6] In it, Menger provided a unique account of economic

---

[6] Importantly, many of the ideas central to Menger's work and that of his followers—including, for example, the emphasis on the role of the entrepreneur—had been hinted at by earlier economists like the nineteenth-century French liberals. Similarly, Menger's emphasis on invisible-hand processes and the un-designed nature of key social institutions derives from the Scottish Enlightenment (e.g. from Hume, Ferguson, and Smith).

behavior, especially of the theories of value and price, which he explained were rooted in the subjective attitudes of individuals. His writings inspired the work of many other notable economists, including Eugen von Böhm-Bawerk, Friedrich von Wieser, Ludwig von Mises, Wilhelm Röpke, F. A. Hayek, Fritz Machlup, Oskar Morgenstern, Ludwig Lachmann, Murray Rothbard, and Israel Kirzner. These economists spanned about four generations of academic economists, and together they formed the core of what is known as the Austrian school. In more recent decades, Mises, Rothbard, and Kirzner in particular, and to a lesser degree, Hayek,[7] Machlup, and Lachmann, directly inspired many younger – mainly American – economists to adopt the Austrian label.[8]

Many other prominent economists have worked in or around the Austrian tradition, including Philip Wicksteed, John Bates Clark, Frank A. Fetter, and William H. Hutt. More recent examples of sympathetic fellow-travelers include British economists G. L. S. Shackle, Jack Wiseman, Brian Loasby, and Stephen Littlechild. And many more mainstream economists have given credit to Austrian school economists for particular ideas. For example, economists as different as Nobel Prize winners Kenneth Arrow, Douglass North, Edmund Phelps, and Oliver Williamson have all praised Hayek's insights about dispersed knowledge.

The most famous name among the economists associated with the Austrian school is that of the brilliant and iconoclastic Joseph Schumpeter. Schumpeter was not a member of the "mainstream" Austrian tradition and was reluctant to be considered a member of any school of thought, but his emphasis on the entrepreneur and historical processes, as well as his skepticism of macroeconomics and his insightful analysis of the role of politics and ideology, places him close to the Austrian camp. At the same time though, his fascination with econometrics and mathematical economics distances him from the Austrians. The work of the great American economist Frank H. Knight (1921) likewise shares some key themes and insights with the Austrian school – notably his emphasis on entrepreneurship and uncertainty – and in our discussion of Austrian perspectives on entrepreneurship we reference some of his most relevant ideas.

---

[7] Hayek's case is somewhat special. As the only Austrian Nobel Laureate, his influence has naturally been enormous. However, his main direct influence on younger economists took place in the 1930s after he became Tooke Professor at the London School of Economics (LSE), a position he held until World War II. However, few of Hayek's many brilliant students and followers at LSE became Austrian economists, and a number of them, notably Abba Lerner and Nicholas Kaldor, in fact became associated with socialist positions.

[8] These include Mario Rizzo, Joseph Salerno, Roger Garrison, Lawrence White, Peter Lewin, Peter Boettke, and their followers and students. Thus, the history of Austrian economics in the United States now spans three generations. On the modern Austrian school, see Vaughn (1994) and Salerno (2002).

Given this colorful cast of characters, it is well to ask what makes Austrian economics unique and valuable. Its first notable characteristic is its scope. Austrian economics attempts to offer a wide-ranging but integrated account of economic relations, with a focus on *realistic* explanations of the *causal* relationships between economic phenomena. In other words, it seeks to understand value, prices, and other economic facts as they exist in the world, rather than how they might behave under highly abstract or unrealistic conditions, such as long-run equilibrium. Austrian economics looks at economic behavior "warts and all", and grapples with difficult problems like the uncertainties and errors that plague human action, and what they mean for society at large. We argue that this emphasis on realism is one reason Austrian work is ideally suited for the study of both theoretical and applied problems in the management disciplines.

It is difficult to reduce Austrian economics to only a few ideas; nevertheless, a limited review of some of its most important contributions is necessary. Austrian economics is most distinct in its approach to "mundane" economic topics, especially "price theory, capital theory, monetary theory, business-cycle theory, and the theory of interventionism" (Klein, 2008a). We choose to focus here on themes that are usually included among the first two of these topics. These themes are: subjectivism, tacit and dispersed knowledge, capital, time and uncertainty, and entrepreneurship. These topics lie at the heart of Austrian approaches to management studies, particularly issues germane to entrepreneurship, strategy, and the theory of the firm. Unpacking them will help underline a vital conclusion that frames much Austrian work in these fields: the market is not a static or equilibrium state, but rather a dynamic process in which individuals use the price system to coordinate their actions and improve their welfare over time. Entrepreneurs play the leading role in this process, which is therefore also a starting point for investigating a wide range of problems in management studies.

Austrian Economics: Key Concepts

Methodological individualism. Austrian economists are often associated with "individualism". However, individualism comes in different forms. Thus, laymen associating Austrian economics with individualism often have *political* individualism in mind, as in the political philosophies of classical liberalism or libertarianism. It is true that many Austrians have been associated with individualism in this sense.[9] However, Austrian economics per se is, as Austrians

---

[9] Not all, however. For example, Friedrich von Wieser and, somewhat later, Richard von Strigl, were not liberals, while Frank A. Fetter was jointly influenced by early progressivism and liberalism.

insist, *"wertfrei"* in the sense of Max Weber: value-free, neutral, and not prescribing any political stance. Indeed, when it is said that Austrian economics is built on individualistic premises, something quite different is meant. Austrians subscribe to *ontological* individualism, that is, the position that ultimately only individuals can truly act. When we routinely ascribe agency to collectives or corporate persons this is an "abbreviation" representing a complex web of interdependent decision-making. The closely related *methodological* position asserts that individuals and the things they perceive, like, plan, do, etc. are the ultimate building blocks of social science. Collectives such firms, groups, divisions, etc. can ultimately only be understood in terms of individual action and interaction. As Menger (1883: 158–59) stated, "[Orders] as a rule are not the result of socially teleological causes, but the unintended result of innumerable efforts of economic subjects pursuing individual interests." In fact, the term *methodological individualism* was coined by Austrian economist Joseph Schumpeter (1908).

Similarly, relations between collective entities ("Chinese tariffs caused the US to respond with tariffs on US produced goods," "the actions of Firm A provoked a reaction from Firm B," "capabilities cause profits", etc.) can only be understood in terms of their underlying patterns of individual action and interaction. This was a major point in Menger's (1883) critique of the German Historical School (particularly of its best-known proponent, Gustav Schmoller). Extreme structuralist positions in sociology, according to which individual action is entirely determined by structural roles, is one articulation of the opposite position of *methodological collectivism*. Since individuals are anonymous occupants of structural roles and are in essence alike, they are of little or no analytical interest, and any attention should center on macro structures. Modern economics, particularly macroeconomics, sometimes also slips into methodological collectivism of this sort. Students of basic Keynesian theory may remember notions of "C", "I", "Y" and other macro aggregates, and somewhat mysterious arguments about how these aggregates are linked through "multiplier" processes (Lachmann, 1969).

In fact, even management theory often makes use of methodologically collectivist arguments. This may come as a surprise, because "management" is usually taken to be, literally, the management of men (and women), clearly a very "micro" activity. Indeed, one of the key founders of modern management theory, Chester Barnard (1938), argued that "management begins always and everywhere with the individual". However, much management theory is as methodologically collectivist as sociology in that it emphasizes structures, practices, routines, capabilities, competencies, and other constructs over the individuals who comprise them. While such collective or aggregate constructs, usually deployed at the level of firms, have their place in management thinking, they are persistently used without clarifying how they relate to individuals' feelings, tastes, plans, etc. In other words, much management thinking is unfortunately, by design or default, not in conformity with the implication of methodological individualism that "we shall not be satisfied with any type of explanation of social phenomena which does not lead us ultimately to a human plan" (Lachmann 1969: 154).

In sum, Austrians subscribe to a "microfoundations" approach. So do most modern economists, of course, but microfoundations can take different forms. Indeed, Austrian microfoundations differ from those of mainstream economists in several key respects. Nevertheless, the Austrian variant based on a methodological individualism, which highlights the plans individuals form in order to pursue their goals, continues to provide valuable foundations for entrepreneurship and management research (McCaffrey, 2018a).

Subjectivism. Austrian economists from Menger onward have emphasized that value is subjective. That is, "value" is not something inherent or objective that exists within a good, but describes a relation between a valuing person and an object being valued.[10] Tastes and preferences differ both between individuals and for the same person over time, and the basic architecture of choice includes many subjective elements. For example, costs and benefits, and the incentives they offer, must ultimately be understood with reference to the subjective views of individuals. The same is true of the foundational economic concept of opportunity cost, which is simply a reflection of a particular person's preference rankings (Buchanan, 1969; Newman, 2018).

The notion of subjective value, though simple, has far-reaching consequences for the way economic theory is developed and applied. In particular, it places the individual consumer at the center of economics. It implies, for example, that the prices of all consumer goods and services, as well as all factors of production (land, labor, capital), can be traced back to individual preferences and to marginal decision-making. The end of all production is consumption, in other words, the creation of value for consumers. And it is with consumer welfare in mind that economic behavior is organized. Value is "imputed" through each stage of production, starting with consumers assessing the worth of final products and continuing until eventually their valuations touch the prices of all factors of production in the economy. The prices of the factors reflect their marginal contributions to the creation of useful final goods for consumers, and

---

[10] While neoclassical economics also incorporates subjectivism in terms of the preferences and (sometimes) beliefs of decision-makers, Austrians embrace a more thoroughgoing subjectivism, as will become clear.

combining and allocating factors is the job of entrepreneurs. Crucially though, the ultimate test of entrepreneurial success lies with consumers, whose decisions to buy and not to buy determine profits and losses. In a competitive market economy, consumers are "sovereign" (Mises, 1949: 270–272; Hutt, 1936).

Tacit and Dispersed Knowledge. Austrians have extended the idea of subjectivism of preferences to include subjectivism of knowledge, information, and expectations. Thus, Hayek (1937, 1945, 1952) famously argued that not only is knowledge dispersed across the multitude of individuals that make up the division of labor, it is also "tacit" and "subjectively held." Thus, the knowledge that matters for economic decisions is mostly idiosyncratic "knowledge of the particular circumstances of time and place" (Hayek, 1945: 521). Such knowledge is experiential (rather than vicarious) and may be difficult to articulate explicitly. As such, it is difficult to transmit to, for example, a central planning board. This insight is the essence of the knowledge-based critique of socialism (Hayek, 1935, 1945), one of two key Austrian lines of thought on the problem of central planning (the other being Mises's entrepreneurial "calculation" argument; Salerno, 1990a, 1990b, 1993). Furthermore, because individuals' knowledge is mainly idiosyncratic and experiential, they typically interpret "the same" information differently (e.g., Hayek, 1952). Hayek's insights formed the basis of Ludwig Lachmann's point that, because they hold different knowledge and different interpretive frameworks, individuals will hold different expectations (Lachmann, 1977). These in turn influence investment, financing, and production decisions, and are thus intimately bound up with the whole structure of the economy.

Austrian ideas about the tacit, dispersed, and subjective nature of knowledge dovetail in many ways with current management thinking. Thus, organizational theory has long understood that the decentralization of organizational structures is dependent on the dispersed nature of knowledge (e.g., Galbraith, 1974). The branch of management theory known as "knowledge management" (Easterby-Smith & Lyles, 2011; Foss & Michailova, 2009) deals with many of the same kinds of questions that informed the "socialist calculation debate" of the 1930s – for example, to what extent can knowledge be centralized in the hands of a planning agency, and what are the barriers to knowledge flows from individuals (individual units) to the agency? Like Hayek (1945), this literature highlights tacit knowledge as a key barrier. The subjectivity of knowledge and expectations are also central to management research. Thus, scholars often stress how organizations may form their interpretive frameworks for making sense of what goes on in their environments (Foss, Klein, Kor and Mahoney, 2008). Such frameworks include what Penrose (1959) called the firm's "image" of the external environment. Another example in contemporary management research is Karl Weick's work on how firms "construct" their environments by "sense-making" processes.

Uncertainty. The process of valuation and want-satisfaction is not automatic or given, because *uncertainty* provides a constant barrier to successful action. Uncertainty is a natural implication of two facts: first, the existence of tacit and dispersed knowledge, and second, the fact that action takes place in time. These factors, especially the temporal character of action, introduce the possibility of incomplete information and error, which lead to the frustration of plans and the waste of scarce resources. However, not all future events are unforeseeable or impossible to cope with, and so it is necessary to introduce a distinction between different types of unknown future events: risks and uncertainties.

Different scholars have different ways of expressing this distinction, but the core differences are that risks are homogeneous, repeatable, and relatively predictable, whereas uncertainties are heterogeneous, unique, and inherently unpredictable. Risks can be mitigated using insurance contracts and similar devices, but uncertainties defy attempts at control. They represent the "unknown unknowns" of the economic world. In fact, we argue that they pose a special problem that requires a particular type of talent to solve, namely, entrepreneurial judgment. The special role of the entrepreneur is to use good judgment to overcome uncertainty, and is the subject of the next section. For the moment though, it is enough to point out that uncertainty is pervasive in all areas of human life, not only in economic affairs or in management contexts. Furthermore, the persistent flow of time means that only temporary equilibria are possible in any market: because the data of the economy are constantly in flux, no long-run equilibrium ever truly exists. It is for this reason that Austrian economic research often stresses the idea of the market as a ceaseless process rather than an end-state.

Several economists have adopted versions of the risk-uncertainty distinction, including Frank Knight (1921) in his concept of "uncertainty," Ludwig von Mises (1949) in his frequentist notion of "case probability," and G.L.S. Shackle (1972) via the idea of "genuine surprise." The main point is that each involves separating an idea of "true" uncertainty from actuarial or probabilistic risk. Foss and Klein (2012, ch. 4) further discuss modern attempts to analyze uncertainty, such as Bewley's (1986, 1989) formal Bayesian analysis. A related literature in management focuses on "judgments and decisions," especially behavioral biases that deviate from the neoclassical economic notion of rationality (e.g., Hastie, 2001).

Heterogeneous capital. Production leads naturally to the problem of *capital*. Although capital is often neglected in mainstream treatments of economic theory, for Austrian economics it is indispensable. Capital – along with land and labor – is one of the basic factors of production familiar to economists, and in this sense, it is not "neglected." However, it is fair to say that "capital theory" has lapsed into obscurity in modern economics, and in microeconomics, and particularly macroeconomics, there is no "view of capital." Modern economics does not really have a theory of capital per se. It has theories of investments and interest, but not a theory of capital in the sense of the Austrian economists, namely, as a set of "intermediate" highly heterogeneous resources that may stand in relations of complementarity, specificity, etc. to each other and can only be treated as a stock under conditions of long-run equilibrium. Instead, modern economics holds a view of capital as a homogeneous mass of inputs. Capital is reduced to a kind of theoretical blob or "shmoo," as Robert Solow referred to it.

Which view of capital one holds matters for understanding phenomena like entrepreneurship, strategy, and organization. Thus, if capital is truly homogeneous, combining and organizing resources is trivial. There are few, if any, problems of management as it is unproblematic to coordinate identical resources. Cooperation problems (e.g., moral hazard and opportunism) are also unlikely to emerge, as it is hard to imagine that asymmetric information is a major issue if resources are similar. And if resources are identical, resource-based competitive advantages cannot exist, by definition. These thought experiments merely serve to illustrate that actual management thinking presupposes heterogeneity on the resource, or capital, side of things. By the same token, a realistic picture of the economic process presupposes a notion of capital heterogeneity.

Conclusions

In sum, Austrian economics strives for a realistic analysis of economic and social relations, beginning with the basic facts of human choice and ultimately building to an explanation of aggregate economic activity and complex social institutions. The wide but practical scope of Austrian work can thus serve as a foundation for research in many fields of the social sciences and business disciplines. The remaining sections of this Element explain a series of ways this is being done, beginning with one further part of Austrian theory, the one that is most fundamental to management studies: the theory of entrepreneurship.

3 Entrepreneurship

The Domain of Entrepreneurship Theory

Entrepreneurship plays a central role in Austrian economics. Ludwig von Mises famously described the entrepreneur as the "driving force" of the market economy, and there is scarcely a major work in the Austrian tradition that does not contain at least some discussion of entrepreneurial behavior. However, there is no "one" Austrian view of the entrepreneur; instead, opinions on the subject are diverse, and can vary widely on many issues, from practical questions about what entrepreneurs actually do on a daily basis to fundamental problems about the purpose of entrepreneurship theory. To avoid confusion about these different strands of thought, we first clarify the domain of entrepreneurship theory, while in the following sections we explore some major themes and points of contention in the literature. We then build on this foundation with a discussion of the *judgment-based approach* to entrepreneurship, which synthesizes and extends many key elements in Austrian work.

It is vital to begin by defining the domain of entrepreneurship theory, as there are several research streams within the academic literature, each with its own methods and units of analysis. Following Klein (2008), we distinguish between occupational, structural, and functional theories.

Occupational theories define entrepreneurship as self-employment and treat the individual as the unit of analysis. They describe the characteristics of individuals who start their own businesses and explain the choice between employment and self-employment (e.g. Kihlstrom a Laffont, 1979; Shaver & Scott, 1991; Parker, 2004). One strand of occupational theories of entrepreneurship is formulated in the language of neoclassical economics and can be considered part of the subfield of labor economics in which the choice between employment and self-employment is a maximizing choice on the margin. Psychological and sociological approaches looking at the personal characteristics of individuals or the effect of social forces on personality, with the goal of explaining why some people and not others choose self-employment, are also occupational in this sense.

Structural approaches treat the firm or industry as the unit of analysis, defining the "entrepreneurial firm" as a new or small firm or a particularly innovative firm. Various literatures on industry dynamics, firm growth, clusters, and networks have in mind a structural concept of entrepreneurship (e.g. Acs & Audretsch, 1990; Aldrich, 1990; Audretsch, Keilbach, & Lehmann, 2005). Structural approaches are common in the economic geography and evolutionary economics research streams.

Functional theories view entrepreneurship as a series of actions, or as a process, rather than an outcome like launching a start-up company (Klein, 2008). These theories may be called "functional" or "system-level" because they highlight the entrepreneur's unique function in the economic system of the market economy. These functions include providing a mechanism that "closes pockets of ignorance" in the market (Kirzner, 1997) by exploiting "hitherto unrecognized" opportunities for earning a "pure profit" (Kirzner, 1973), thus driving the market process toward an equilibrium; injecting new products, processes, etc. into the economic system (Schumpeter, 1934); or, setting up new firms that allow the entrepreneur to deploy assets and investments in the pursuit of profit under uncertainty (Knight, 1921). Such theories are a foundation of the activity-based, processual research trend in entrepreneurship studies (Shepherd, 2015; McCaffrey, 2018a), and are also the subject of this section. Many different types of actions have been used to define the entrepreneurial function, including small-business management, imagination or creativity, innovation, alertness to opportunities, the ability to adapt to change, charismatic leadership, and judgment (Foss & Klein, 2012: 30–41). While valuable research exists on each of these topics, our focus will mainly be on entrepreneurial judgment and related concepts.

Austrian Contributions to Entrepreneurship Theory

Austrian theorizing about entrepreneurship began in Menger's foundational *Principles of Economics*, which outlined four possible functions entrepreneurs could perform:

> (a) obtaining information about the economic situation; (b) economic calculation – all the various computations that must be made if a production process is to be efficient (provided that it is economic in other respects); (c) the act of will by which goods of higher order (or goods in general – under conditions of developed commerce, where any economic good can be exchanged for any other) are assigned to a particular production process; and finally (d) supervision of the execution of the production plan so that it may be carried through as economically as possible. (Menger, [1871] 1985: 68])

This passage reveals that Menger imagined a wide scope for entrepreneurial behavior, which is one reason later Austrians were able to develop his ideas in a variety of ways. He indicates the need for entrepreneurs to survey available possibilities for production, grapple with uncertainty by gathering information, commit scarce resources to the most important projects, and eventually bring the process to completion. But at the core of Menger's account of the entrepreneur is the idea of taking action to guide production in an economical way (Martin, 1979).

Menger's theory was further developed by his students Eugen von Böhm-Bawerk and Friedrich von Wieser.[11] Böhm-Bawerk's research mainly focused

---

[11] The first systematic attempt to develop an Austrian theory of entrepreneurship was made by one of Menger's earliest students, Viktor Mataja, in a now-forgotten book titled, *Der Unternehmergewinn. Ein Beitrag zur Lehre von der Güterverteilung in der Volkswirtschaft*, or, "Entrepreneurial Profit: A Contribution to the Doctrine of the Distribution of Goods in the National Economy" (1884).

on capital and interest theory, but he sought to clarify some essential points about entrepreneurship as well. He was especially interested in extending Menger's ideas about subjectivity and uncertainty to the theories of production and distribution (Böhm-Bawerk, 1962). As part of this larger goal, he noted the importance of entrepreneurial foresight in guiding production. He concluded that the entrepreneur's function involves a specific type of action and decision-making:

> [E]ven if he does not personally participate in the labor of production, he contributes a certain measure of personal effort, either by reason of the intellectual effort represented by his supervision, or by his formulating policies for the business to follow, or at the very least because of the act of will by which he determines that his means of production shall be enlisted in the service of that particular enterprise (Böhm-Bawerk, 1959: 6).

Böhm-Bawerk also provided a basis for integrating capital into the theory of entrepreneurship. In other words, the role of decision-maker in a firm implies control over the use of scarce resources, especially capital goods, which are used over time. Guiding production means entrepreneurs must make decisions about how best to allocate heterogeneous capital goods among competing uses. If they do this successfully, they earn profits and increase the value of their capital, and if not, they earn losses and must eventually surrender their decision-making authority to competitors. A key point is that entrepreneurship generates a unique type of income, namely, profit or loss, which is different from the wages, interest, and rent that accrue to other economic actors (McCaffrey & Salerno, 2014).

Friedrich von Wieser also made important contributions to Austrian economics. His work mainly involved elaborating Menger's value theory, and among other things, he is known for popularizing the terms "marginal utility" and "opportunity cost" in economics. He also made remarks about the entrepreneur's economic function, which he presented as an eclectic mix of ownership, management, leadership, innovation, organization, and speculation. He believed that the entrepreneur "must possess the quick perception that seizes new terms in current transactions as his affairs develop" (Wieser [1914] 1927: 324). This remark is significant because it hints at the idea of entrepreneurship as alertness to opportunities later developed by Israel Kirzner. In general though, Wieser depicted entrepreneurs as innovators, describing them as "Great personalities ... bold technical innovators, organizers with a keen knowledge of human nature, far-sighted bankers, reckless speculators, [and] the world-conquering directors of the trusts," daring individuals driven by "the joyful power to create" ([1914] 1927: 327).

Wieser's theory and rhetoric strongly influenced Joseph Schumpeter, whose work on entrepreneurship was the most successful to emerge from turn-of-the-century Vienna (McCaffrey, 2013). Schumpeter was trained by the Austrians but considered himself independent of any school of thought. Nevertheless, he adopted some important themes from Wieser's work, including his dramatic theory of the entrepreneur as a kind of industrial hero who constantly reshapes the economy through innovation and "creative destruction," an idea that continues to influence management research (Schumpeter, 1934, 1942).

The work of the early Austrians proved influential outside their native country. In the United States, for example, economists like John B. Clark, Herbert J. Davenport, and Frank A. Fetter also worked out many implications of Austrian price theory, including the theory of entrepreneurship. Fetter in particular is notable for his early development of the idea of entrepreneurial judgment (Fetter, 1915, 1936), and he provided a detailed account of entrepreneurship and its relation to the firm that remains relevant to this day (McCaffrey, 2016). Like other economists working in the Austrian tradition, he pointed out the need for a special kind of decision-making to overcome the uncertainties of production, which he realized extended far beyond simple risks. As he put it, "The risk of business is not that of the throwing of dice in which (if it is fair) skill plays no part and gains in the long run offset losses. Business risk is rather that of the rope-walker in crossing Niagara" (Fetter, 1915: 369).

Only the exercise of good judgment, a kind of developed decision-making skill, can safely overcome uncertainty. Fetter thus explains entrepreneurial success and failure as the result of specific choices entrepreneurs make. This is in sharp contrast to theories of entrepreneurship based on serendipity or luck. Fetter did of course acknowledge that not all circumstances are under the entrepreneur's control; however, he suggested that whenever luck and choice are set side by side as explanations of profit and loss, the role of luck is often exaggerated. In his words, the "more the causes of success in general are studied, the larger is found the element of choice, the smaller that of luck" (Fetter, 1915: 360). What is perceived as luck often turns out to be simply good judgment.

Austrian theories of entrepreneurship received their fullest elaboration in the work of Ludwig von Mises, whose contributions are still considered foundational by contemporary Austrians. Mises assigned entrepreneurs a central role both in the market process and in economic theory generally. Like his predecessors, he stressed the necessity of bearing uncertainty, which is the special function of entrepreneurs. However, he also explained the vital social role of entrepreneurship and of the profit and loss system in coordinating economic action and increasing public welfare. In Mises's view, under a system of private property and the division of labor, the guiding principle of economic activity is consumer sovereignty. Entrepreneurs may govern their own enterprises, but they are ultimately beholden to consumers, whose decisions make them rich or poor. Successful entrepreneurs earn profits, which signal that they are using scarce resources effectively to satisfy demand. Unsuccessful entrepreneurs earn losses, which symbolize a failure to properly anticipate consumer wants. The profit and loss system thus functions as a selection mechanism that rewards those entrepreneurs who excel at improving the welfare of their customers (Mises, 1949, [1951] 2008).

For Mises, entrepreneurship is a defining characteristic of the market economy. However, entrepreneurs require specific institutional conditions if they hope to successfully use the resources at their disposal to satisfy consumers. The most important of these institutions is the price system. Mises argued that market prices are indispensable tools that allow entrepreneurs to guide production in the most economical way. Prices expressed in money terms enable entrepreneurs to appraise the costs and benefits of different plans that will come to fruition only in the future. Such "economic calculation" by entrepreneurs is the fundamental fact of the market economy. In fact, a freely-operating system of money prices is the only way entrepreneurs can compare and make sense of the seemingly-infinite number of production plans available to them (Mises, [1920] 1990b). This insight lies at the heart of Mises's critique of central planning: without market prices, there is no way for the planners to assess the costs and benefits of their production decisions, much less choose the most beneficial ones (Salerno, 1990b). Central planning effectively abolishes entrepreneurship and rational economy, while prices and economic (entrepreneurial) calculation coordinate action across time and space and systematically improve human welfare by allocating resources to their most urgent needs.

Alertness and Discovery

Recent work in Austrian economics draws on a range of entrepreneurship theories, each of which can be traced to the ideas of Menger and the early Austrians. A particularly noteworthy example in terms of its impact on contemporary entrepreneurship research is the theory of entrepreneurial alertness pioneered by Israel Kirzner (1973, 1979, 1985; Klein & Bylund, 2014), whose concept of entrepreneurial discovery was first outlined in his landmark *Competition and Entrepreneurship* (1973). Building on Hayek's theories of knowledge and competition, Kirzner argues that entrepreneurship is best thought of as alertness to previously-unnoticed profit opportunities. His theory is first and foremost an explanation of market-clearing; in other words, it explains how the discovery of profit opportunities leads the market toward equilibrium. Opportunities emerge any time that prices, quantities, or qualities diverge from their equilibrium values. When they do, "alert" individuals can earn a profit by exploiting knowledge to bring supply and demand into harmony. This can occur in different ways, including through simple price arbitrage and by perceiving the need for a product or service before others do. Entrepreneurs in this view are discoverers; they discover new resource uses, products, markets, and possibilities for arbitrage – in short, opportunities for profitable exchange. And by closing pockets of market ignorance, entrepreneurship always stimulates a tendency toward equilibrium.

In the past two decades or so Kirzner's work has become a major inspiration of the "opportunity discovery" approach to entrepreneurship (Shane, 2003; Shane & Venkataraman, 2000). In this conception, the study of entrepreneurship is seen as centering around three research questions, namely why, when, and how (1) entrepreneurial opportunities arise, (2) certain individuals and firms and not others discover and exploit opportunities, and (3) different modes of action are used to exploit those opportunities (Shane & Venkataraman, 2000: 218). This is an ambitious and sweeping research program; yet, in practice, research within it mainly considers the antecedents of opportunity discovery associated with start-ups.

The opportunity recognition or discovery view has also been subjected to a number of criticisms. The most fundamental relate to the notion of opportunity, which is often treated as the defining characteristic of entrepreneurship studies as well as its unit of analysis. Yet we believe this program has only been somewhat successful at developing its agenda, and that the emphasis on opportunities is partly to blame.

Consider the following question: what is it that entrepreneurs discover or create? In Kirzner's (1973, 1997) formulation, price differentials (spatially or temporarily) create what are essentially arbitrage opportunities. The "alert" entrepreneur spots and seizes these objectively existing opportunities before other actors. The purpose of Kirzner's theory, however, is not to explain entrepreneurial action per se, but to offer a macro-level account of market equilibrium; if alert entrepreneurs are present, waiting to exploit profit opportunities resulting from disequilibrium, this disequilibrium cannot last for long (Foss & Klein, 2010). Oddly, Kirzner's "pure entrepreneur" does not own any assets (Rothbard, 1985; Salerno, 2008). He has no interest in teams or in firms. Uncertainty plays no role in this account, because opportunities are objective and known as soon as they are discovered, and there is no possibility of loss, because there is no investment (the worst that can happen is that an entrepreneur fails to recognize an opportunity, neither gaining nor losing). In fact, there is little role for action and decision-making of any kind, as entrepreneurs stumble upon opportunities rather than search for them systematically (McCaffrey, 2014a). There is no explicit attempt to systematically disentangle the discovery, evaluation, and exploitation of opportunities. Thus, the entrepreneur in Kirzner's theory should not be mistaken for the real thing; it is a device used to explain equilibration.

Of course, management scholars building upon Kirzner's ideas have added their own psychological, experiential, demographic, or network-related factors to the explanation, typically as antecedents of opportunity discovery (e.g., Shane, 2000; Gaglio & Katz, 2001; Choi & Shepherd, 2004; Ardichvili, Cardozo, & Ray, 2003; Baron & Ensley, 2006). But the resulting theories share key features of Kirzner's approach. In particular, while there is a growing literature dealing with opportunity evaluation (e.g., Keh, Foo & Lim, 2002; Wood & Williams, 2014) and exploitation (e.g., Choi, Levesque & Shepherd, 2008; Hmieleski & Baron, 2008; Godley, 2013; Godley & Casson, 2015), the initial act of recognition or discovery continues to receive the lion's share of attention.

The main empirical manifestation of entrepreneurship, in this approach, as well as in entrepreneurship research in general, continues to be the act of starting a new company. In contrast, there is much less interest in understanding how *established* firms engage in the discovery, etc. of opportunities (Foss & Klein, 2012). These latter phenomena are typically seen as falling outside the study of entrepreneurship proper, and are studied in neighboring fields such as corporate entrepreneurship or "intrapreneurship." The main emphasis also continues to be on the individual entrepreneur rather than the entrepreneurial team (see, further, Foss & Lyngsie, 2014).

These biases may partly derive from measurement issues. Thus, focusing on the discovery or recognition of an opportunity by an individual means that the exercise of entrepreneurship is located at a point in time (Dimov, 2007). In contrast, if entrepreneurship is a messy process involving the interaction of many individuals with more or less concrete ideas and experimenting with available resources and different ways of sourcing them ("evaluating" opportunities) – attempting to arrive at something more definite ("exploiting opportunities"), as in the effectuation approach (Sarasvathy, 2008) – measurement is much more complicated. If furthermore these processes take place within a complex hierarchy, measurement may become even more difficult. However, we argue that it is ultimately the emphasis on "opportunity" that produces the above biases (and the more so, the more the "objective" nature of opportunities is stressed).

The Judgment-Based Approach

A major strand of Austrian entrepreneurship theory is the judgment-based approach. This view is based especially on the work of economists like Knight, Mises, and more recently, Rothbard. The judgment-based approach starts with the fact of judgment – the need for individuals to make decisions about the future without access to a formal model or decision rule, as would apply to situations of "rational" behavior under probabilistic risk. Without access to such a model, the decision-maker uses intuition or gut feeling (Huang and Pearce, 2015), or what Mises called *Verstehen*, or "understanding." For Mises, and to a lesser extent Knight, the exact mechanisms of judgment, the behavioral and cognitive processes by which entrepreneurs form their beliefs about future conditions, are a black box. Mises (1949: 582) says the entrepreneur relies on a "specific anticipative understanding of the future," one that "defies any rules and systematization." As Casson (1982: 14) notes, "[t]he entrepreneur believes he is right, while everyone else is wrong. Thus, the essence of entrepreneurship is being different – being different because one has a different perception of the situation."

The idea of entrepreneurial judgment is thus rooted in the microfoundations discussed in Section 2. In particular, the judgment-based approach begins with the subjective values and knowledge of individual entrepreneurs and examines the way they inform action and decision-making as they attempt to successfully navigate a complex and uncertain environment. Judgment is exercised by resource owners, who combine productive assets under conditions of uncertainty (Foss & Klein, 2012). As Ludwig Lachmann (1956: 16) put it: "We are living in a world of unexpected change; hence capital combinations ... will be ever changing, will be dissolved and reformed. In this activity, we find the real function of the entrepreneur." Entrepreneurship is thus not merely a perceptive behavior such as idea generation or creative thinking, but the act of taking responsibility for real assets, investing them in anticipation of uncertain future rewards. As Knight (1921) famously argued, to exercise such responsibility, the actor must put resources in play – that is, must establish and operate a business firm. Hence, the theory of entrepreneurship and the theory of the firm are two sides of the same coin. Entrepreneurship also carries more "macro" implications: entrepreneurial judgment is an irreducible element of comparative advantage, and therefore plays an indispensable role in determining trade patterns and international specialization among firms (Dorobăț & Topan, 2015).

Another implication of asset ownership is that entrepreneurship is inextricably linked with questions of property-rights and other fundamental social institutions. This insight is a vital part of Mises's theory of economic calculation

(Machaj, 2007). In fact, entrepreneurship research has long recognized the "embedded" nature of entrepreneurship and institutions. Most importantly, institutional forces influence the quantity and the quality of entrepreneurship by determining the "rules of the game" in which entrepreneurs operate (Baumol, 1990). Different rules support and incentivize different types of judgment, not all of which are beneficial for society at large. Depending on the prevailing institutional setup, entrepreneurship can be "productive" in the sense of promoting consumer welfare and wealth-creation, or it can be channeled into "unproductive" or "destructive" activities such as rent-seeking and organized crime (McCaffrey, 2018b).

In the policy sphere, the institutional foundations of judgment also provide grounds for skepticism regarding the likely success of government regulation of entrepreneurial activity. In particular, if regulation creates uncertainty surrounding key business decisions or disturbs the price system, it multiplies the problems entrepreneurs face while at the same time crippling their ability to deal with them effectively (Higgs, 1997; McCaffrey, 2015a; Bylund & McCaffrey, 2017).

Boundaries of Entrepreneurial Judgment

Any theory of entrepreneurial decision-making requires an account of its limits. At what point does it become impossible for entrepreneurs to use good judgment? To answer this question, it is helpful to contrast judgment with *luck*. We view luck as a type of pure chance that is completely beyond the control of any given individual, and therefore is an extreme boundary to decision-making. At the other end of the choice spectrum are perfectly defined decision rules that remove the need for deliberation and choice altogether. Judgment occupies the space between these extremes.

Luck is not studied systematically in the entrepreneurship literature, but the idea lurks in the background of several theories, often as a criticism. Harold Demsetz (1983), for example, challenged Kirzner's notion of opportunity discovery by asking how, analytically, discovery can be distinguished from luck. Given Kirzner's emphasis on spontaneity and surprise, and his idea that opportunities cause their own discovery without search efforts, it is hard to conclude that it can be (Kirzner, 1985; McCaffrey, 2014a). Schultz (1980: 439) raised a similar question, putting it this way:

> [I]t is not sufficient to treat entrepreneurs solely as economic agents who only collect windfalls and bear losses that are unanticipated. If this is all they do, the much vaunted free enterprise system merely distributes in some unspecified manner the windfalls and losses that come as surprises. If entrepreneurship has

some economic value it must perform a useful function which is constrained by
scarcity, which implies that there is a supply and a demand for their services.

The key to understanding Schultz's challenge is to recognize his rejection,
following Friedman & Savage (1948), of the concept of Knightian uncertainty.
If all uncertainty can be parametrized in terms of (subjective) probabilities, then
decision-making in the absence of such probabilities must be random. Any
valuable kind of decision-making must be modelable must have a marginal
revenue product, and must be determined by supply and demand. For Knight,
however, decision-making – what Knight calls judgment – is not random, and it
simply cannot be modeled by a set of formal decision rules. It does not have
a supply curve because it is a residual or controlling factor that is inextricably
linked with resource ownership. It is a kind of understanding or *Verstehen* that
defies formal explanation but is nevertheless rare and valuable.

Without the idea of Knightian uncertainty, then, Knight's concept of
entrepreneurial judgment makes little sense. Indeed, in our view the prime
challenge to incorporating judgment into mainstream economics is the profes-
sion's general unease with Knightian uncertainty. Despite some useful
attempts to model it formally (see Foss & Klein, 2012, ch. 4), most economists
remain uncomfortable with something like judgment, which lies between
"rational", articulable decision-making and random behavior. Fortunately,
management and entrepreneurship research have no such hang-ups, one reason why research on cognition and decision-making is thriving in these
disciplines (e.g. Shepherd, 2015).

Conclusions

The theory of entrepreneurship is an indispensable part of Austrian economics.
Although there are different strands of Austrian thinking on the subject,
throughout this Element we emphasize the importance of viewing entrepreneurship as judgmental decision-making. This perspective has deep roots in the
Austrian tradition, which also stresses the notion of economic calculation –
entrepreneurial judgments are usually made in the context of market exchange
and money prices, which entrepreneurs use to guide their decisions about how
best to use scarce, heterogeneous capital goods. However, judgment and economic calculation are relevant in many institutional settings. In fact, they are
keys that unlock countless doors across different fields of management research,
including market and non-market organization, strategy, and the theory of the
firm. The next section extends the judgment-based approach by applying it to
unconventional business ventures and even to organizations entirely outside the
traditional marketplace.

4 Extensions of Entrepreneurship Theory

Introduction

Theories of entrepreneurship tend to conform to the maxim that "the business of business is business." That is, entrepreneurship research has historically focused on commercial activity, and on one question in particular: where do business profits (and losses) come from? Many possible answers have been suggested, including innovation, alertness, and uncertainty-bearing, but a persistent assumption of all these views is that the entrepreneur's proper or only place is in the marketplace. However, this assumption has been recently challenged by scholars who attempt to apply insights from conventional entrepreneurship research outside the boundaries of the business world, thereby creating a series of sub-fields of research that we classify under the heading of *alternative entrepreneurship* or *non-market entrepreneurship*. In this section, we explain how Austrian ideas can be applied in three of these areas: social entrepreneurship, political entrepreneurship, and institutional entrepreneurship.

Social Entrepreneurship

Entrepreneurship research tends to focus on profit-seeking entrepreneurs and the organizations they create and govern. This is also true in Austrian economics, which is especially interested in contrasting entrepreneurship in the market economy with decision-making under socialist central planning. This contrast formed the basis of Mises's and Hayek's critiques of socialism, for example. However, Austrian views of entrepreneurship and economic calculation can also be used to analyze a wide range of activities that fall outside strictly for-profit enterprise or socialist central planning. These include organizations in the voluntary market economy that are not intended to compete on the market with the primary goal of earning monetary profits, such as charities, cooperatives, trusts, mutual societies, social enterprises, and other entities that might be considered "not-for-profit." Sadly, the exact functions of these organizations, as well as their significance for entrepreneurs, are often obscured by vague or superficial rhetoric, which prevents robust economic analysis. Nevertheless, understanding calculation within these organizations – or the lack thereof – allows us to appraise their true costs and benefits, the role they play in the economy, and their ultimate impact on society.

The increasingly popular business form known as *social entrepreneurship* provides an example. Social enterprises are typically defined as business organizations that do not narrowly pursue monetary profit and returns for shareholders, but rather aim to create value for stakeholder groups by providing solutions to "social" problems (Harding, 2004; Martin & Osberg, 2007).[12] Social problems are in turn defined as basic human needs that are unmet by prevailing market and political institutions (Seelos & Mair, 2005). In practice, this means social entrepreneurs use business ventures to directly and indirectly transform disadvantaged or marginalized communities, especially those affected by low levels of education and high levels of poverty, unemployment, homelessness, injustice, etc. (Alvord, Brown & Letts, 2004; Martin & Osberg, 2007; Abu-Saifan, 2012). The positive outcomes created by social organizations are referred to as "social value" (Seelos & Mair, 2005; Haugh, 2006; Peredo & McLean, 2006; Dacin, Dacin, & Matear, 2010). According to Bloom (2012: 73) social value,

> can emerge in the ways the products or services of the venture function; the ways they are distributed and delivered; the advocacy approach of the venture; the ways the venture accumulates and deploys financial, human, and other resources; or the ways the venture's networks or partnerships are configured.

Explained this way, social entrepreneurship seems straightforward enough. Yet a deeper look at the literature reveals a number of ambiguities regarding the economic meaning of social enterprise. Fortunately, these can be resolved by using the Austrian framework outlined in the previous sections.

The most important example of confused or ambiguous meaning in the social entrepreneurship literature relates to the word "social" itself. This term is used to qualify countless others in entrepreneurship studies, and as a result, its meaning has become obscured if not completely destroyed.[13] Thus, social enterprises are said to create "social value" by building "social capital" that is used to make "social investments" that produce a "social return on investment" and encourage "social innovation" in order to solve "social problems." In these examples and many others, the word social is used to transform standard economic terms into metaphors that reflect the special objectives of non-traditional business organizations.

However, these metaphors often imply a false conflict with traditional entrepreneurship. For example, the contrast between conventional market entrepreneurship and social entrepreneurship implies that the former is somehow not social, or even anti-social. This is misleading, however; for example, Austrians would respond that Mises's calculation argument demonstrates that the

---

[12] Cf. Zahra et al. (2009) and Dacin, Dacin, and Matear (2010) for a survey of different definitions of social entrepreneurship. Although the term is often used loosely and inconsistently, our approach is compatible with many current definitions.

[13] It is unsurprising that "social" is often combined metaphorically with another metaphorically used term, "capital," to form the doubly vague "social capital."

entrepreneurial market economy is profoundly social. Entrepreneurs, by bearing uncertainty in an effort to satisfy consumers, work ceaselessly to improve the welfare of all members of society, and their work in turn strengthens bonds of cooperation between individuals and communities, while at the same time disincentivizing conflict and exploitation. This is social behavior in its most fundamental form.

A related problem concerns "social value." This term is not inherently flawed, but is prone to misunderstanding because it indicates a different type of value from the kind entrepreneurs typically create for consumers. Of course, if social value simply indicates the fact that businesses create positive externalities, it is harmless enough. The main conceptual danger arises when discussion of social value leads to methodological collectivism – when it is taken to mean that value exists for society as such, independent of the values of its members. The trouble with this view has been hinted at already in Section 2: the Austrian subjective theory of value demonstrates that there is no separate social value distinct from the ordinary values of individuals. Rather, value, whether it is called economic or social, indicates a relationship between individuals and the world, specifically, a perceived causal relationship between a plan of action and the satisfaction of a need. There is therefore no value that is not contained within a human mind. The above are just two examples of ambiguous terms in the social entrepreneurship literature. Yet by applying Austrian insights, they can be made more consistent and useful for management research.

Austrian theory has more to say about social entrepreneurship than its terminology, however; it also provides a robust framework for thinking about social enterprises and their organization. Although social ventures come in many different shapes and sizes, they all must grapple with some basic economic problems. Taking on a special social mission besides simply earning profits does not relieve them of the pressures of the marketplace, because social enterprises are fundamentally business organizations. That is, they aspire to be independent of charitable and governmental support (Dees, 1998), and in theory at least, they earn revenue through the sale of goods and services rather than through donations or public grants (Emerson & Twersky, 1996). Therefore, like traditional entrepreneurs, social entrepreneurs must use judgment to allocate scarce resources in the face of uncertainty (Mort, Weerawardena, & Carnegie, 2003; Peredo & McLean, 2006). Furthermore, genuine participation in the market as commercial entities (and not just as charities) means they are still subject to the profit and loss test. Social enterprises must be mindful of costs and of consumers' values if they are to remain viable. Simply choosing not to make profit-seeking the main goal of the enterprise does not mean it is unnecessary to hazard scarce resources in the marketplace. Neither can social entrepreneurs avoid making use of heterogeneous capital assets, whose market values influence the ability of the enterprise to fulfil its mission.

Consider a hypothetical example: a social enterprise sells sandwiches and donates all its profits to a local homeless shelter. The mission cannot be successful without actually generating profits, which in turn means consumers will have to value its sandwiches highly enough to cover the costs of its business while leaving enough left over to support the social side of the enterprise. A key implication is that what entrepreneurs decide to do with their profits – keep them as personal income or give them away – does not change the economic necessities of running their businesses.

This leads naturally to questions about the social firm and its boundaries. If social enterprises are subject to the profit and loss test, do they also require access to the price system, as conventional businesses do? The answer is yes. As explained in Section 6, ordinary businesses require external prices in order to establish the boundaries of their firms. Without such prices, they become "islands of calculational chaos" (Rothbard, 1962: 1364) unable to estimate the costs and benefits of production. Social ventures differ from this requirement only in degree, not in kind. In particular, they employ unique and previously-unpriced factors of production, especially labor (Dacin, Dacin, & Matear, 2010). As a result, they are more prone to calculation errors to the extent that they allocate resources without the price system to guide them. As Klein observes, "innovation carries with its benefits the cost of more severe internal distortions" (Klein, 1996: 17). The most reliable cost estimates come from mundane businesses, because these organizations strive hardest to appraise prices correctly. Social enterprises will therefore be most efficient in sectors where ordinary entrepreneurs have established a well-developed network of prices that can be used to estimate implicit costs. However, it is not always possible to find such a network in practice because some social business customers find it difficult to pay even the minimum required prices (Mair & Marti, 2006). In consequence, social enterprises often exist on the boundaries of the price system. The economist Frank Fetter remarked that entrepreneurs take "the more exposed frontier of risk" (Fetter, 1915: 347). Along similar lines, we might say that social entrepreneurs take the more exposed frontier of economic calculation.[14]

Austrian insights into economic calculation and judgment also apply to more complex forms of social enterprise where the business and the social mission are integrated and inseparable. For example, suppose the sandwich company

---

[14] This fact explains why social enterprise is sometimes less attractive to prospective entrepreneurs than conventional business: social enterprises are more prone to failure due to calculation problems, and this danger is not necessarily offset by the prospect of increased returns.

mentioned above hires some unemployed homeless persons as cooks. In this case, the goal of the enterprise is not simply to increase profits to support an external mission, but to achieve multiple, sometimes conflicting goals. It may be the case that a homeless employee lacks the skills and productivity that would normally be required in a competitive labor market in the same industry, but that his social enterprise employer wishes to keep him on all the same. There is thus a conflict between the profitability and long-term survival of the enterprise and its short-term mission to help its employees. The venture now faces a trade-off between efficient decision-making and *gift-giving*. To the extent that they insist on making unprofitable decisions, entrepreneurs step outside the sphere of economic calculation: they strategically choose certain departments (or products) in their businesses that are not subject to the profit and loss test. Lacking this guide, some departments will tend to produce inefficiently, and social entrepreneurs will have no choice but to subsidize them using the profits from more successful ones. In conventional business, poor performance encourages entrepreneurs to scale back failing departments and increase production in more profitable lines; in social enterprise, keeping an inefficient division alive is often a vital part of the mission. This point is consistent with empirical research showing that social enterprises tend to sacrifice monetary profits in order to expand consumption among their target groups (Agafonow, 2015), and also with the more general idea that all people try to maximize psychic profit, but not necessarily monetary profit (Mises, 1949: 287; Rothbard, 2009: 71–72).

It is not always easy in practice to separate efficient economic action from gift-giving. As Mises (1949: 242) explains,

> The boundaries between buying goods and services needed and giving alms are sometimes difficult to discern. He who buys at a charity sale usually combines a purchase with a donation for a charitable purpose … Man in acting is a unity. The businessman who owns the whole firm may sometimes efface the boundaries between business and charity. If he wants to relieve a distressed friend, delicacy of feeling may prompt him to resort to a procedure which spares the latter the embarrassment of living on alms. He gives the friend a job in his office although he does not need his help or could hire an equivalent helper at a lower salary. Then the salary granted appears formally as a part of business outlays. In fact it is the spending of a fraction of the businessman's income. It is, from a correct point of view, consumption and not an expenditure designed to increase the firm's profit.

Once again, economic calculation acts as a boundary on social entrepreneurs' choices. The greater the number of decisions that entrepreneurs make outside the sphere of economic calculation, the more inefficient their businesses will become. In the most extreme case, every decision is treated as social, and there is no scope for economic calculation at all. In this case the social enterprise essentially becomes a conventional charity. We can infer from this that if entrepreneurs want to effectively deliver on their promises to alleviate social problems, they will strive wherever possible to use the price system so as to limit inefficiencies as much as possible. They can then focus their attention on a small number of non-calculable decisions that deliver the bulk of the social value generated by their enterprises. But the overarching problem is that no social enterprise can expand its social mission to the point that prices, for all products, disappear.

Political Entrepreneurship

The boundaries of entrepreneurship theory are also being pushed to include actions and organizations altogether outside the market. The most important type of this research involves political institutions. The growing field of *political entrepreneurship* asks question like: to what extent are political actors willing and able to act in an entrepreneurial way? What are the similarities and differences between entrepreneurship in the market and in the political realm?

The concept of the political entrepreneur derives mainly from public choice economics and political science but is also expanding within entrepreneurship studies as such (Klein et al. 2010; McCaffrey & Salerno, 2011). It is based on the premise that political behavior does not exist in an economic vacuum, and that some of the main problems market entrepreneurs struggle to solve also appear in government organizations. For example, governments are owners of heterogeneous resources and exert some kind of ultimate control and decision-making about how to use them. Likewise, scarcity and uncertainty exist across all institutional settings, meaning that judgment in some form must be exercised in government: some agency must combine resources and bear some immediate consequences. We call this government decision-making function political entrepreneurship.

Despite some superficial similarities, however, political and market entrepreneurship are not the same. At least three main differences exist, each of which creates unique problems for public decision-makers. First, traditional methods of public finance – taxation, borrowing, and inflation – are not directly voluntary, and stand in sharp contrast to the methods used by market entrepreneurs, who depend on attracting interested investors and paying customers. Second, public decision-makers do not run competitive businesses operating within the price system, and therefore lack access to economic calculation. Related to this, third, governments are not subject to the profit and loss test – and ultimately to bankruptcy and elimination – if they fail to satisfy their "customers." In other words, governments face many of the same resource-allocation decisions as market entrepreneurs, while lacking the vital institutional framework to successfully solve them. Governments are in a sense "islands of calculational chaos" that exist alongside market economies.

Entrepreneurial judgment and economic calculation can thus provide a framework for analyzing the methods and practice of political decision-making, and for comparing its welfare outcomes to those of alternative institutional arrangements. However, applying the framework is challenging. Probably the most important obstacle is identifying the locus of control and ultimate decision-making within political organizations. This is straightforward enough in the case of absolute monarchies or totalitarian dictatorships, which embody clear hierarchies and chains of authority, but far more difficult in modern representative democracies. Untangling the web of original and derived judgment, and of political entrepreneurship and political proxy-entrepreneurship, becomes tremendously complex in these kinds of states. Matters are even more confused when considering the relations between the democratic elements of government and the more bureaucratic governance structures that often make up a large part of modern states' regulatory regimes.

Entrepreneurship and the Rules of the Game

Another more general strand of entrepreneurship research explores the relations between entrepreneurial action and institutions. This line of work is usually credited to William Baumol, whose 1990 paper "Entrepreneurship: Productive, Unproductive, and Destructive" helped launch a wide research stream devoted to the role of entrepreneurs in promoting economic growth, or their failure to do so (Baumol, 1990). Baumol's insight was simple, but powerful: entrepreneurship happens within a given institutional framework. Economic activity is governed by a system of rules that determines the relative rewards to different types of action. These rewards channel entrepreneurial talent into activities that yield the greatest relative payoffs. If prevailing institutions make it profitable to satisfy consumers in the marketplace, entrepreneurs will throw their efforts into productive activity, and the result will be wealth-creation and economic growth. However, if the rules incentivize other behaviors that are not socially beneficial, growth will be slowed or even reversed. By changing the relative payoffs to different actions, entrepreneurial talent is thus redistributed into "unproductive" or "destructive" activities like rent-seeking and organized crime.

Although valuable, Baumol's approach is open to several 'productive' criticisms, starting with his theoretical foundations. Baumol mainly adopts

Schumpeter's definition of entrepreneurship as a creative, innovative activity in the pursuit of wealth, power, and prestige (Baumol, 1990: 897–898, 909). The trouble is that this theory takes no account of *uncertainty* (Rothbard, 1987; McCaffrey, 2009), and it is no surprise that Baumol passes over this issue as well. Yet uncertainty is vital for a working definition of entrepreneurship, because without it, there is no possibility of entrepreneurial *failure*. And without failure, we must assume that entrepreneurs automatically succeed in acting according to the rules of the game, always achieve their goals, and always obtain the highest relative rewards. Yet the entrepreneurial environment – whether productive, unproductive, or destructive – is filled with uncertainty. Rent-seekers can waste money lobbying for legislation that is never passed, a Mafioso can mistakenly appraise the future demand for illicit substances, and courtiers can spend small fortunes seeking patronage that never materializes. Entrepreneurs constantly hazard scarce resources while working toward a perceived benefit, whether productive or not. In fact, unproductive and destructive entrepreneurs of the past used complex arrangements of heterogeneous physical and other capital to pursue their goals. The possibility of failure is an ever-present threat to entrepreneurs of all types, and any realistic theory of the allocation of entrepreneurial talent must take this fact into account.

In any case, entrepreneurs are not passive with respect to institutions: they have some ability to choose how to respond to institutional constraints. Likewise, they do not passively receive rewards and punishments, but actively play a role in determining what they are and whether they are successfully captured. Entrepreneurs do not compare certain rewards available to them in the present; instead, they compare uncertain future returns that they believe will result from their own actions in the present. This insight is missing from Baumol's analysis, which focuses on the simple choice between productive, unproductive, and destructive action, and takes success in these roles as given.

This hints at a further question: success *compared to what?*[15] That is, what benchmark can we use to distinguish between productive and unproductive entrepreneurship, and how do we measure entrepreneurial success in either? Finding answers requires looking beyond the equilibrium-focused theory of Schumpeter to alternative frameworks such as the Austrian theory of the market process.

For economists like Mises, entrepreneurial decision-making is a forward-looking attempt to anticipate consumer demand (Salerno, 1993). Entrepreneurs

---

[15] This is also a key question posed by Lucas and Fuller (2017).

bid for and combine heterogeneous capital goods that they devote to production over time (Foss et al., 2007), and only when the final output appears on the market do entrepreneurs discover if their judgments about the prices of the factors of production were correct. If they are, entrepreneurs earn profits and demonstrate productivity in the sense of accurately assessing consumers' valuations of the factors. If not, entrepreneurs earn losses and are eventually eliminated from the market, thereby signaling errors in their appraisal of the value of the factors, and thus the unproductive or destructive use of scarce resources (Mises, 1949, [1951]2008). The Austrian theory thus defines productivity via the selection mechanism of the market process: unproductive entrepreneurship is a systematic waste of resources (especially capital goods) and a corresponding failure of entrepreneurs to satisfy the most urgent wants of consumers. Once 'embedded' in this theory, Baumol's productive, unproductive, and destructive typology becomes a way to consider entrepreneurs' decisions in terms of their practical outcomes for consumers. In doing so, it meets the challenge posed by some of Baumol's critics (Davidson & Ekelund, 1994), who argue that his welfare benchmark fails to account for uncertainty.

Institutional Entrepreneurship

Baumol's basic point about institutions is widely accepted, but it describes only one part of a more complex relationship between entrepreneurs and institutions. Crucially, Baumol assumes the institutional framework is simply given to entrepreneurs, who respond to it mechanically by choosing the type of entrepreneurship that carries the greatest relative rewards (McCaffrey, 2018b). However, a growing body of research argues that this assumption is unrealistic and unnecessary. In fact, it may even confuse the issue by ignoring a key possibility, namely, that entrepreneurship can influence the institutional setup in addition to being influenced by it.

In the wake of this criticism a literature on *institutional entrepreneurship* has developed to explain other types of entrepreneurial action with respect to "the rules of the game." This research has been recently advanced, for example, by Douhan & Henrekson (2010), who take an important step forward by expanding Baumol's classification of entrepreneurial behavior. Their key insight was that entrepreneurs can be "institution makers" as well as "institution takers." As opposed to a binary choice between productive and unproductive action, entrepreneurs choose across three different types of institutional behavior: abiding, evading, and altering (Henrekson & Sanandaji, 2011). Abiding entrepreneurship occurs within the constraints of existing institutions, evasive entrepreneurship circumvents institutions, and altering entrepreneurship works to actively change the institutional framework. Each of these three forms of entrepreneurship can be productive or unproductive. The range of possible entrepreneurial actions is thus expanded from two to six.[16]

The expanded typology helps to show more clearly that entrepreneurs are not simply at the mercy of the rules of the game. Instead, entrepreneurial action takes on new significance as a vital explanation of institutional persistence or change. This framework also offers wide scope for analyzing entrepreneurial behavior inside and outside traditional firms and markets, and it provides a natural complement to key themes in Austrian economic theory. In particular, uncertainty plays a vital role in the expanded typology of behavior: decisions to abide by, evade, or alter institutions must be made in advance, with no guarantee of success. Entrepreneurs must judge which types of action will yield the greatest relative results, and they can, and often will, be mistaken. For example, some will successfully evade regulatory measures through black markets or use altering tactics to capture regulators, but many will fail as well. Entrepreneurs' individual, subjective perceptions of the available payoffs are therefore just as relevant as any objective distribution of rewards.

The institutional entrepreneurship framework also raises many questions and challenges. For instance, we have emphasized the importance of the heterogeneity of entrepreneurial skills, and this issue is relevant also for comparing entrepreneurial performance across institutional environments. It seems unlikely that entrepreneurs can use their judgment equally well in radically different settings, for example, when founding a business firm and launching a political movement. In fact, entrepreneurs are not equally skilled in all contexts (Engelhardt, 2012), and there are significant costs involved in switching between abiding, altering, and evading action (Bylund & McCaffrey, 2017).

More could also be said about the cause-and-effect relationships between different types of entrepreneurship. For example, if entrepreneurs alter political institutions, say by removing stifling regulations, how does this affect the relative payoffs to abiding and evading action, or the rewards to further altering? Policy questions also become more complex in light of the new typology. What if a poorly-designed policy encourages evasive entrepreneurship, but also inspires technological breakthroughs that are integrated into abiding entrepreneurship and are responsible for widespread social benefits? As with Baumol's theory, the question arises of how to benchmark the welfare analysis of entrepreneurial action. And once again, the Austrian approach, which emphasizes the welfare of consumers as the ultimate end of production, is ideally suited to provide an answer.

---

[16] Or nine, if Baumol's original category of destructive entrepreneurship is included.

There is also room for discussion of the boundaries institutions place on entrepreneurial judgment, and the problems entrepreneurs face in trying to use their judgment to overcome them. To take only one example, there are likely to be limits to the effectiveness of altering entrepreneurship, especially when it comes to transforming fundamental institutions like cultural norms, which change infrequently (Williamson, 2000; Bylund & McCaffrey, 2017).[17] As explained below in Section 6, the boundaries of the firm are set in part by entrepreneurs' access to external prices (through the process of economic calculation). What decision-making boundaries exist for entrepreneurs acting in the broader institutional environment outside traditional firms? Intuitively, it is reasonable to suppose that there are hard limits on entrepreneurs' abilities to successfully evade or alter every institution in society; at some point, the complexities and uncertainties simply become too great, especially without a guide such as the price system to use in navigating them.

Conclusions

Although entrepreneurship is mainly studied in the context of business activity in a market economy, the key elements of entrepreneurial judgment exist in many other areas of society as well. This section discussed a few of the ways that Austrian economics, especially the theories of economic calculation and judgment, can add to our understanding of how entrepreneurship governs and transforms a variety of organizations and institutions, ranging from experimental and not-for-profit firms, to political organizations, to the institutional environment in general.

5 Strategy in an Entrepreneurial Perspective

Austrian Influences on Firm Strategy

The dictionary definition of strategy is "a plan of action designed to achieve a long-term or overall aim." Historically, the origins of strategy lie in the theory and practice of planning and directing overall military operations and movements in a war or battle. Thus, strategy is about winning or doing better than someone else, and is therefore an inherently relative or comparative enterprise. In the theory and practice of management, strategy finds its origins in thinking at the Harvard Business School after World War II (Christensen, Andrews) on "business policy" as the "integration" of the various functions of the company. Another source is practitioner-driven thinking in the 1960s on long-range

---

[17] In addition to acts of deliberate change, a large amount of research has been conducted under the label of "institutional work" that examines the roles of involuntary and experimental entrepreneurial action in institutional transformation.

planning and portfolio approaches to managing the diversified company associated with firms such as the Boston Consulting Group. Academically, strategy was established as a discipline toward the end of the 1970s, the landmark event being the founding of the *Strategic Management Journal* in 1980 and the publication the same year of Michael Porter's *Competitive Strategy*.

Contemporary strategy research in management addresses competitive heterogeneity, that is, why firms competing in the market process (notably firms in the same industry) realize different financial returns.[18] Over the last few decades, this has crystallized into a concern with *sustained competitive advantage* as the key phenomenon of strategy research. Actions, behaviors, plans, etc. are "strategic" to the extent that they somehow have implications for sustained competitive advantages. Thus, strategies may be defined as the concrete plans senior managers construct and deploy to achieve such advantages.

A firm is said to be in possession of a sustained competitive advantage when it has the potential to create and appropriate more value than the competition on a persistent basis. In this view, strategy is about creating, maintaining, defending, renewing, etc. competitive advantages, and strategies are more or less formal plans or patterns of actions that ultimately aim at this. Strategy scholars typically think of strategies as hierarchical. In this hierarchy, corporate strategies (what are the markets in which we want to compete or be present?) are the highest-level manifestation of strategy, followed by competitive strategy (how do we want to compete in the markets we have decided to compete in?), and then functional strategies (particular plans for functional units that may contribute to business unit or to corporate-level sustained competitive advantage). The field is a major, established, and influential one in modern management research.

While the work of Hayek, Schumpeter, and (to a lesser extent) Kirzner have become standard references in the management literature on entrepreneurship (cf. Section. 3), there is relatively little direct Austrian influence on the strategy field. To be sure, there have been some developments in studies of, for example, competitive dynamics (Young et al., 1996), entrepreneurial top-management teams (Foss et al. 2008), and the tangled links between rents and costs (Lippman & Rumelt, 2003; see also Lewin & Phelan, 2000). Some key Austrian and semi-Austrian contributions are also sometimes cited in strategic management, notably Schumpeter (1934), Hayek (1945), and Kirzner (1973). However, overall the direct influence of the tradition remains very limited, at

---

[18] There is also strategy research in a military context; conflict theory addresses various aspects of strategy and mathematics-based game theory similarly grapples with strategic problems. Of these, it is mainly game theory that has had an influence on strategy research in management. See, for example, Ghemawat (2002).

least if compared to the influence of, for example, transaction cost economics (Williamson, 1985) or, more broadly, industrial organization on the strategy field.

However, as Jacobson (1992: 782) noted, "Industrial organization largely ignores, despite their importance, change, uncertainty, and disequilibrium in the business environment. Because these fundamental characteristics are cornerstones of the Austrian School of Economics, this doctrine offers unique strategic perspectives." We are **sympathetic** to this overall assessment. Thus, the basic contention of this section is that the firm's key strategic decisions – strategy formulation, market analysis, industry positioning, diversification, vertical integration and outsourcing, organizational design – are ultimately entrepreneurial decisions. That is, they are about the best possible stewardship of scarce, heterogeneous capital resources under conditions of uncertainty in the pursuit of profit. As we argued in the preceding section, these decisions are determined by the application of judgment. Judgment takes place in established companies through new strategies or revising existing ones. This exemplifies the point made earlier that judgment and the exercise of judgment in entrepreneurship are not reserved for start-ups; they are a general aspect of decision-making under uncertainty.

While the direct influence of Austrian economics on strategy thinking is limited, we argue that a more active infusion of core strategy thinking with key Austrian ideas will help further both. In particular, Austrian ideas on judgment under uncertainty in the context of a complex capital structure dovetail with key currents in contemporary strategy thinking while also adding new insights to them.

The Resource-based View: The "Austrian School of Strategy"?

Strategy scholars typically make a key distinction between the analysis of market structure and other aspects of the firm's external environment, and the analysis of its internal activities and resources. The familiar "five forces" framework associated with Porter (1980) is almost exclusively dedicated to the first kind of analysis, while the resource-based view (RBV) is mainly dedicated to the second. We here summarize the essentials of the RBV (see Foss & Stieglitz, 2011, for a more extensive discussion).

The resource-based view. The RBV derives its name from its fundamental claims that competitive advantage is rooted in the resource endowment of the firm. Early seminal statements of the view are Demsetz (1972) and Lippman and Rumelt (1982) in economics, and Wernerfelt (1984) and Barney (1991) in management research.[19] These early contributions have given rise to so much subsequent influential work in strategy that the RBV is arguably the dominant view in the field. Thus, while much current strategy discussion may revolve around notions such as "dynamic capabilities" or "competences," these notions capture particular kinds of resources, and much of the currently highly influential "dynamic capabilities view" is basically an attempt to 1) take the RBV in a more dynamic direction based on 2) theorizing particular kinds of resources.

"Resources" are not always clearly defined in the literature (e.g., they are sometimes defined as "inputs" that are tied to the firm on a "semi-permanent" basis or as "anything that can be thought of as a competitive advantage to a firm"). Resources are, however, simply inputs. It is intuitive that some inputs are trivial in terms of performance implications for the firm (e.g., paper clips) while others certainly are not (e.g., a highly dedicated engineering capability). To sort the wheat from the chaff in the analysis of competitive advantage, as it were, RBV scholars have developed various lists of jointly necessary criteria that a resource must conform to if it is to be a source of competitive advantage. The most familiar one is probably the "Value, Rarity, Inimitability and Non-substitutability" (VRIN) framework associated with Jay Barney. As Barney (1991: 102) explains

> A firm is said to have a competitive advantage when it is implementing a value creating strategy not simultaneously being implemented by any current or potential competitors. A firm is said to have a sustained competitive advantage when it is implementing a value creating strategy not simultaneously being implemented by any current or potential competitors and when these other firms are unable to duplicate the benefits of this strategy.

In this scheme value may be linked to the existence of a span between the reservation price of the products made possible by the relevant resource and the opportunity costs of production of those products.[20] Rare is to be understood in a simple counting sense (i.e., it is not the same as economic scarcity), implying that not "too many" other firms can implement the same strategy. The two last criteria refer to the cost of imitating or substituting the resource or bundle of

---

[19] While often heralded as the founding contribution to the RBV (and bearing several Austrian imprints, perhaps through the influence of Penrose's advisor, Fritz Machlup), Penrose's (1959) analysis of the growth process of the diversifying literature is not really a contribution to the analysis of competitive advantage. We return to Penrose's analysis later in this section.

[20] Barney (1986) establishes the necessary condition for sustained competitive advantage that resources are acquired or rented at a price lower than their net present value. If they are not, any competitive advantages will be offset by supply prices on "strategic factor markets." This is explicitly included in Peteraf (1993), who also introduces a condition of relative immobility of resources. If resources are perfectly mobile they will be able to muster the bargaining power that will lead them to appropriate all the value they create.

resources that give rise to the competitive advantage. These costs should be prohibitive.

The "Austrian School of Strategy"? In an article published in arguably the most prestigious journal in management research, the *Academy of Management Review*, Robert Jacobson (1992) discussed what he called the "Austrian School of Strategy." He associated this "school" with the then-emerging RBV influenced by scholars like Edith Penrose, Richard Rumelt, Birger Wernerfelt, and Jay Barney. To Jacobson, what made the RBV "Austrian" in flavor was the alleged emphasis of the RBV on change, uncertainty, and disequilibrium, themes that are indeed closely associated with Austrian economics. Unfortunately, Jacobsen went too far in identifying the RBV as an Austrian-based approach (Foss, 2000). Although in some key respects, the RBV is reminiscent of central Austrian themes (e.g., the importance of local knowledge, resource heterogeneity), it is essentially based on the Marshallian (neoclassical) theory of firms and markets as set out in intermediate microeconomics textbooks (see, e.g., Peteraf, 1993; Peteraf & Barney, 2003), and in particular the twists and tweaks such microeconomics received at the University of Chicago and UCLA in the hands of able price-theorists like Harold Demsetz and Armen Alchian. Thus, the emergence of the RBV does not reflect any influence of Austrian work per se, but rather a realization by many strategy scholars that strategy had neglected to pay sufficient attention to the internal side of firms, including the resources they own, access, and control, and how these are deployed and protected to maximize rents over time.

Thus, the RBV (Lippman & Rumelt, 1982; Barney, 1991; Peteraf, 1993) is built upon the neoclassical model of perfect competition and the production-function view of the firm, but with significant variations (Foss & Stieglitz, 2011). More specifically, the core RBV model (Lippman & Rumelt, 1982; Peteraf, 1993) postulates an environment with many competing firms within the same industries that have different productive efficiencies (think of this as having different average cost curves). Thus, some firms will realize a return to their superior efficiency in the form of a "rent," typically analyzed as a Ricardian scarcity rent. This rent can be sustained over time if the causes of superior performance are costly to imitate – either because of their inherent characteristics (e.g., if they are complex or tacit) or costly to substitute in the sense that the same rent-yielding strategies can be implemented with a different resource-bundle (Barney, 1991). Clearly, this is a timeless equilibrium model that examines the conditions under which rents are sustainable in equilibrium. Its closest Austrian cousin is what Mises called the "evenly rotating economy" (Mises, 1949).

In contrast, Penrose's (1959) approach to firm capabilities and firm growth shares more with Austrian and evolutionary concepts of the firm and market than with neoclassical economics or the modern RBV (Barney, 1991; Peteraf, 1993). Her key idea is that it is not resources per se that determine what a firm does and how it develops (e.g., in terms of broadening its product portfolio through related diversification), but rather the services that can be extracted from resources. These, in turn, are determined by what top-management envisions can be done with the firm's resource-base as guided by the "image" (Penrose, 1959) it holds of the firm's internal and external environments and how this influences its perception of its "productive opportunity set." Thus, firm performance is directly linked to mental representations held at the top-management level. Foss et al. (2008) argue that in many respects this is akin to the subjectivism of Austrian economics, but it is a subjectivism that, rather than being placed at the level of the individual decision-maker, appears at the level of the (senior management) team.

And yet, in some key ways, the RBV is closer to core Austrian themes than many other approaches to strategy, notably those based on industrial organization economics, whether the structure-conduct-performance view of the post-War decades (e.g., Bain, 1956) or more recent game theory-based industrial organization economics (cf. Waldman & Jensen, 2016). Here are some of the characteristics of the RBV that support a reading of it as at least congenial to Austrian theory.[21]

First, the RBV highlights that performance differences can ultimately be traced to heterogeneity of the resource bases that firms control. This is closely related to the Austrian emphasis on heterogeneous, yet specific and complementary capital goods (Lachmann, 1956, 1977). Superior profitability is seen as emerging from bundles of resources, with different resource bundles associated with different efficiencies. As a consequence, resource-based scholars think of firms as bundles of heterogeneous resources, assets, or activities. These assets have different (economic) life expectancies. Such unique and specialized assets can also be intangible, such as worker-specific knowledge or firm-specific capabilities (Barney, 1986; Dierickx & Cool, 1989). These assets can be specific

---

[21] Foss and Stieglitz (2011) argue that the RBV is "a half-way house": on the one hand, it has revitalized the concern with firm heterogeneity, innovation, and dynamics associated with more heterodox economics, while on the other hand, the core RBV model (Demsetz, 1973; Lippman & Rumelt, 1982; Barney, 1986, 1991; Peteraf, 1993; Peteraf & Barney, 2003) is a competitive equilibrium model with heterogeneous firms. Other commentators speak of "high-church" and "low-church" versions of the RBV (Gavetti & Levinthal, 2000) (cf. also Matthews, 2006, 2010).

to certain firms and "co-specialized" with other assets such that they generate value only in certain combinations (Teece, 2009). Further, resource- and knowl-edge-based scholars often emphasize that heterogeneous assets per se do not give rise independently to competitive advantages. Rather, it is the interactions among these resources – their relations of specificity and co-specialization – that generate such advantages (e.g., Teece, 1986; Dierickx & Cool, 1989; Barney, 1991; Black & Boal, 1994). These interactions, coupled with path-dependent outcomes of past strategic investments in heterogeneous resources (Nelson & Winter, 1982), imply that heterogeneity, rather than homogeneity, is the hallmark characteristic of resources and firm organization of these resources.

Second, the RBV is fundamentally about specialization and local knowl-edge. Thus, notions of "capabilities," "competencies," etc., also associated with resource-based thinking, may be seen as firm-level manifestations of the kind of localized knowledge that Hayek (1945) in particular emphasized.[22]

Third, the RBV stresses that informational advantage is the ultimate source of competitive advantage. Thus, according to the "strategic factor markets argu-ment" (Barney, 1986), a necessary condition for competitive advantage is that at least one key resource underlying a strategy has been purchased on an input market (a "strategic factor market") at a price that is below its net present value. The interesting issue is not this simple truism, but *what* may cause prices and net present values to diverge. Barney (1986) argues that, supposing that rationality and competitive conditions obtain, the only explanations can be luck or superior information (on the buyer side). Firms may have an informational advantage when it comes to resource value – when the relevant resources form a part of a new value-creating strategy – and the supply side cannot ascertain how and how much the resource in question contributes to this value creation (or simply does not know). Rumelt (1987) explicitly links this to entrepreneurship under Knightian uncertainty.

Fourth, the RBV is an efficiency-oriented perspective on strategy. In the RBV, the superior financial returns that result from competitive advantages represent efficiency rents, that is, returns from innovating more, having better process technology, serving customers in a better way, and so on. Contrast this with the

---

[22] On the other hand, "capabilities," "competencies," etc. are also examples of collective constructs that do not have clear foundations in individual action and interaction (cf. Felin & Foss, 2005; Abell, Felin, and Foss, 2008). In fact, much strategy thinking has a streak of methodological holism, explaining firm-level outcomes in terms of collective notions such as "capabilities" with little or no reference to individuals and their interactions, and as such not conforming to the methodological individualism advanced by Austrians.

emphasis of those perspectives on strategy founded on a market power-view of economic activities (notably Porter, 1980), in which competitive advantage is associated with monopoly rents and the loss of economic welfare. The Austrian view on consumer sovereignty as an ultimate arbiter in the market process and its emphasis on welfare-improving market outcomes (even if the Austrian notion of "welfare" may differ from that of mainstream economics) is much more aligned with the RBV than with those strategy perspectives that are based on, in the final analysis, the monopoly model of market power of basic economics textbooks.

How Austrian Economics Furthers Contemporary Strategy Thinking

While there are areas of overlap between dominant currents in strategy and Austrian economics, Austrian ideas have only been imperfectly absorbed in current strategic management thinking. Thus, Austrians may argue that much strategy thinking is based on equilibrium models. The emphasis in the core models is on identifying the conditions under which resources may yield rents in equilibrium. Causal models that address the process issues of creating new resources, engaging with competitors (outside of equilibrium), forming new expectations, and so on are, if certainly not absent, then in short supply and in general left for more informal discussions. Recognizing the imperfect overlap between strategic management and Austrian work may, however, be taken as a call for more fully drawing on Austrian ideas in strategic management.

In particular, the entrepreneurial approach outlined in the previous sections has implications for firm strategy. As we have argued, entrepreneurship is not simply another resource, like physical and financial capital, reputation, human capital, technical know-how, and the like. Entrepreneurship is a higher-level coordinating and decision-making factor. Our approach suggests that the basic explanation for the key issue of strategy – why there are systematic, long-lived differences in firm-level performance – boils down to entrepreneurs differing in how well they exercise original judgment and delegate derived judgment. The ability to identify and put together resources is itself a capability, albeit of a distinctly entrepreneurial kind (Denrell et al., 2003; Foss & Klein, 2012).

In the following we briefly discuss these ideas in terms of how 1) Austrian capital theory furthers our understanding of resource heterogeneity; 2) judgment serves as the ultimate foundation of competitive advantage; 3) the exercise of judgment allows us to understand the dynamics of the boundaries of the firm (e.g., changing patterns of diversification and vertical integration); and 4)

Austrian ideas provide a take on the strategy process that links up with ideas associated with Henry Mintzberg, Robert Burgelman, and others.

Austrian capital theory and coping with complex resource heterogeneity.
Austrians emphasize that not only is capital heterogeneous, capital is also arranged in a *structure* (Lachmann, 1956) or *system*. As Austrians have also stressed, this structure is a complex one, and the Austrian interpretation of greater capital-intensity or "roundaboutness" is not just the traditional notion of "capital-deepening" (i.e., the K/L ratio is increasing), but also that the structure includes an increasing number of capital goods with more complex interactions. "Interactions" are understood in terms of relations of complementarity and specificity between capital goods and their owners (Hayek, 1941; Lachmann, 1956). Imagining and trying out new combinations of heterogeneous capital goods, or "resources," within such a structure is a fundamental task of the entrepreneur exercising judgment (Foss & Klein, 2012).[23] As Lachmann (1956: 3) notes, "[t]he 'best' mode of complementarity is ... not a 'datum.' It is in no way 'given' to the entrepreneur who, on the contrary, as a rule has to spend a good deal of time and effort in finding out what it is." Relatedly, research within the behavioral theory of the firm (Cyert & March, 1963; Nelson & Winter, 1982) also stresses that optimal technology is not a given; in fact, firms may only know a small part of their "objective" production possibilities and will have to engage in search to discover better combinations of inputs.

There is also a striking similarity between the Austrian capital-based view of entrepreneurship and the theory of complex systems (Simon, 1962; Kauffman, 1993). Herbert Simon (1962) defines "complexity" as a large number of parts that "interact in a nonsimple way" (1962: 468). Simon famously introduced a distinction between "the interactions *among* subsystems on the one hand, and the interactions *within* subsystems (i.e., among the parts of those subsystems) on the other" (1962: 473). Hence, his distinction between *decomposable* systems, in which the interactions among the subsystems are negligible; *non-decomposable* systems, in which the interactions among the subsystems are essential; and *nearly decomposable* systems, in which the interactions among the subsystems are weak, but not negligible (1962: 129). As Langlois (2002) suggests, there is an epistemological dimension to this: the epistemological

---

[23] In a sense, the entrepreneur engages in "search" within a structure, although the "search" metaphor can be misleading as it indicates that the entrepreneur searches through some objectively given structure (rather than imagined and not yet tried combinations of capital goods; Kirzner, 1967).

problem of comprehending a complex system is eased when the system is decomposable or nearly decomposable.

Thus, capital structures (at the firm level) that are close to the non-decomposable end of the spectrum may be particularly hard to comprehend. To use jargon from later complexity research (e.g., Kauffman, 1993) – an increasingly influential current in strategic management and organization theory – the "landscape" of combinations of elements may have multiple peaks. A landscape is a mapping of how combinations of certain entities perform in terms of some metric. For example, the landscape may describe how various combinations of capital goods map into (appropriable) monetary values. Finding the optimal (highest) peak in such a landscape is far from trivial because entrepreneurs cannot survey the entire landscape, that is, they cannot, for reason of bounded rationality and imagination, ascertain and appraise all those combinations of heterogeneous capital goods that may be high in value appropriation. The problem is further complicated when it is recognized that interdependencies and the number of choice variables are not given (as in formal "NK-models" of complex systems; Levinthal, 1997); rather, interdependencies between capital goods are entrepreneurial choice variables.[24] Thus, rather than searching over one landscape, entrepreneurs may be searching over multiple landscapes with different topologies. On the other hand, in highly decomposed systems, the landscape may be single-peaked, so that even simple search strategies (e.g., "gradient search") may quickly reach the peak.

Theory suggests that different landscapes have different properties with respect to how the topology influences search. Thus, when interdependencies are few and weak, there will be few high-performing local peaks, and perhaps only one, relatively low, global peak. Entrepreneurs searching in such a landscape are likely to eventually hit the highest peak (as gradients are smooth), although this may take considerable time. When interdependencies are strong and many, there will be many local peaks, and one global peak that is likely to be very high. Entrepreneurs may quickly reach a peak, but it may be a local, relatively low one, and it may be difficult to escape from it.

So far, complexity theory has not been linked explicitly to entrepreneurs and to the various characteristics of entrepreneurs. While judgment may be inherently impossible to formalize, still, some characteristics of the entrepreneur may influence his or her judgment. For example, we would expect characteristics,

---

[24] As Rivkin (2000), a key contributor to this research stream, points out: "In the formal models described here, managers take N and K as immutable. In reality, managers make investments to build connections across decisions or to sever links ... Loosely coupled organizations ... are responsive to change, but vulnerable to imitation. A natural implication ... is that designers of organizations must decide which they fear more: inertia or imitation" (Rivkin, 2000).

often mentioned in the entrepreneurship literature in general, such as risk and loss aversion, experience, confidence, and so on to be systematically related to the entrepreneur's exercise of judgment in searching over landscapes defined by various capital combinations. Entrepreneurs who are relatively less risk averse and more experienced (and therefore more likely to be more confident) are more likely to engage in search in highly complex landscapes and search for the highest peaks within them.

Entrepreneurial judgment and competitive advantage. If capital could be described as "shmoo," the above "landscapes" would be entirely flat, as any combination of shmoo capital would be as good as any other. In such a world, entrepreneurship would be trivial. However, while heterogeneous capital seems to be a necessary condition for the existence of the entrepreneurial function we have described in the preceding section, it is not sufficient.

Suppose capital is indeed highly heterogeneous, but markets, including intertemporal markets, work perfectly (as in Debreu, 1959). In this admittedly extreme setting, all possible combinations of capital goods are priced, and all prices perfectly reflect scarcities (Denrell, Fang & Winter, 2003). However, this means that there would be no need for entrepreneurs. After all, judgment is the manifestation of speculative appraisals, in the absence of given future prices, of which combinations of capital will yield a profit (Mises, 1949). There would be no need for any search in the landscape of combinations of capital goods, as prices would indicate the highest peaks. This is what Lippman and Rumelt (2003: 1982) call "full strategic equilibrium," which maximizes surplus across the set of all possible assignments of all possible resources to all possible tasks.[25] There would be no role for competitive advantage either. Hence, Lippman and Rumelt (2003: 1085) argue that "the heart of business management and strategy concerns the creation, evaluation, manipulation, administration, and deployment of *unpriced* specialized resource combinations."

Austrian economics shows why Lippman and Rumelt's argument about competitive advantage arising from the exercise of entrepreneurial judgment over the unpriced combination of heterogeneous capital assets is exactly right: under dispersed knowledge (Hayek, 1948), genuine uncertainty (Knight, 1921; Mises, 1949), and sheer ignorance (Kirzner, 1973), current prices *cannot* reflect all combinations of complementary capital goods, that is, all their "multiple specificities." Under these circumstances, some combinations are simply not

---

[25] Lippman and Rumelt (2003: 1982) note in passing that "[t]he number of such combinations, in the real world, is literally noncomputable. The idea that firms actually operate at the maximum within this space is not credible."

imagined by any entrepreneur (Shackle, 1972). Markets that can price such combinations therefore logically do not exist.

Entrepreneurial experimentation and corporate strategy. Complex systems theory suggests that in rugged landscapes (i.e., there are many peaks of varying heights), entrepreneurs may end up on local rather than global peaks. They may regret this – but are stuck. Additionally, Austrian theory suggests that because capital goods are combined under genuine uncertainty, entrepreneurs may misunderstand the true nature of the landscape; what they thought was a peak (i.e., a valuable combination of capital goods) is actually a valley (i.e., combining the capital goods is not profitable), causing regret. In fact, given the dynamic economic reality portrayed in Austrian economics, the landscape of complexity theory is an evolving one; what was a global peak yesterday may be a deep valley today. In such a setting, ongoing entrepreneurial experimentation with capital combinations – new resource bundles – is required, experimentation that is steered by the entrepreneur's mental model (Gavetti & Levinthal, 2000), or what we have called judgment, which may be refined as the entrepreneur searches the landscape (Siggelkow & Levinthal, 2003).[26]

The other side of new "combinations of capital goods" is changes in the boundaries of the firm, as firms seek access, or drop access, to complementary resources through markets, hybrid arrangements, or ownership (Williamson, 1985). In other words, corporate strategy – the choice of the markets where the firm wants to have some kind of presence – reflects entrepreneurial judgment as it pertains to firm boundary decisions in the vertical (i.e., relations to suppliers as well as customers) and horizontal (i.e., horizontal integration and diversification) decisions. Austrian economics can illuminate these dimensions of strategy in a unique manner.

Thus, consider the puzzle that while corporate restructuring creates value on average (Jarrell, Brickley, & Netter, 1988; Andrade, Mitchell, & Stafford, 2001), many mergers are later "reversed." Reversals take the form of divestitures, spin-offs, or carve-outs. From the point of view of agency theory, they can indicate that entrenched managers at some point made acquisitions to increase their own power, prestige, or control. As shareholders assume control or the firm is acquired by another company, these inefficient acquisitions are divested. In this perspective, not only were the acquisitions inefficient *ex post*, but also *ex ante* (Montgomery, 1994). In the very different judgment view though, unprofitable acquisitions may well be "mistakes" *ex post*; however, poor long-term

---

[26] Denrell, Fang and Winter (2003) argue that entrepreneurs stumble upon resource combinations by serendipity. Entrepreneurial search is guided by prior access to idiosyncratic resources rather than by a forward-looking mental representation of the landscape.

performance does not indicate *ex ante* inefficiency (Klein & Klein, 2001). Rather, all a divestiture may mean is that entrepreneurs have updated their forecasts of future conditions. As Mises (1949: 252) puts it, "the outcome of action is always uncertain. Action is always speculation." Consequently, "the real entrepreneur is a speculator, a man eager to utilize his opinion about the future structure of the market for business operations promising profits" (Mises, 1949: 585).

The firm itself – its emergence, boundaries, and structure – can also be understood as a kind of experiment, subject to frequent revision (Mosakowski, 1997; Boot, Milbourn, & Thakor, 1999; Matsusaka, 2001). Entrepreneurs may not know, *ex ante*, how their capabilities, experiences, and other resources apply across products, industries, and markets; to find out, they need to try out different activities and investments. For example, firms may diversify into new industries even knowing that their acquisitions are likely to be reversed. The very process of trying out different combinations provides information that is useful for understanding what the firm can do. We discuss this further in the next section.

Strategy and planning. The dynamic view of strategy that an Austrian perspective suggests includes not just the formation, possible renewal, and eventual destruction of competitive advantages, but also includes the strategy *process*. Strategy scholars often make a distinction between strategy process research and strategy content research. Whereas the latter is taken up with the actual content of strategy (e.g., which generic strategy to pursue, positioning, how to defend a competitive position, how to protect competitive advantages, and so on), strategy process research addresses the process through which organizations formulate the strategies that they may or may not follow in the pursuit of competitive advantages. In the first couple of decades of its existence (i.e., the 1960s and 1970s) strategic management was dominated by a rationalist planning and design ideal, since then associated with the work of Igor Ansoff (1965). Although it may border somewhat on caricature, the ideal was that of a top decision-maker in possession of a clear and transparent corporate objective function, armed with all relevant data, and working out the optimal course of action for the company for a future whose uncertainty could be handled through scenarios and contingency planning. As such, this ideal was of course part of a broader post-War planning optimism.

However, it is also easy to see how this vision resembles the ideal of resource allocation promoted by socialist economists in the interwar period and strongly criticized by Mises and Hayek in particular. An early debate in the *Strategic Management Journal* between two heavy-weights of strategic management,

Ansoff and Henry Mintzberg, (Mintzberg, 1990, 1991; Ansoff, 1991) illustrates exactly this point.

Mintzberg (1990) initiated the debate by an attack on the "design school" in strategic management, represented by Ansoff (1965). This "school" views strategy "as one of design to achieve an essential fit between external threat and opportunity and internal distinctive competence" (Mintzberg, 1990: 171). One may think of this as the familiar SWOT model made concrete. Without mentioning Hayek, Mintzberg's critical arguments against the "design school" are nevertheless distinctly Hayekian. Thus, Mintzberg takes issue with such (alleged) underlying premises of the school as the notion that strategy formation should be an explicitly controlled process of thought; that the CEO is the strategist; that strategies must be fully formulated and be fully explicit; and that implementation presupposes that strategies are, as it were, "complete." Thinking of strategy in this way is reminiscent of what Hayek (1973) called "constructivist rationalism," that is, the notion that only institutions that can have their relevant premises understood to substantiate a rational syllogism can be justified. And like Hayek (1945), Mintzberg (1990: 182) strongly stresses the distinction between practical, explicit knowledge and fleeting, subjective, often tacit knowledge acquired through learning by engaging with an environment: "Our critique of the design school revolves around one central theme: its promotion of thought independent of action, strategy formation above all as a process of *conception,* rather than as one of *learning.*"

The parallels to Hayek's thought become even more apparent when Mintzberg seeks to identify the conditions under which an organization "tilts" toward the design school model of strategy-making (Mintzberg, 1990). He identifies four such conditions, namely

> 1. One brain can, in principle, handle all of the information relevant for strategy formation ... 2. That brain has full, detailed, intimate knowledge of the situation in question. The potential for centralizing knowledge must be backed up by sufficient access to, and experience of, the organization and its situation to enable the strategist to understand in a deep sense what is going on. ... 3. the relevant knowledge is established and set before a new intended strategy has to be implemented – in other words, the situation is relatively stable or at least predictable ... 4. the organization in question is prepared to cope with a centrally articulated strategy (Mintzberg, 1990: 190: emphasis removed).

These conditions are the same ones Hayek identified as underlying comprehensive socialist planning (Hayek, 1945). Condition (3) mirrors Hayek's (1948) point that dynamics make concentrating knowledge even more challenging and (4) basically refers to implementation problems of the mechanism design variety that have also been highlighted as a challenge to centralized resource allocation. Strangely, Mintzberg seems to be unaware of the parallel; at any rate, there is no mention of Hayek in his article.

In a rather temperamental response, Ansoff (1991) seeks to provide counter-examples to Mintzberg's many critical points against planning and design approaches to strategy. He then tries to attack Mintzberg's view of strategy as an emergent process involving experimentation, and contrasts this view with the "rational model of learning": "The age of enlightenment ushered a new model which recognized importance of cognition in the affairs of man. In this model decision-making is the first stage, followed by implementation of the decision. It became the standard model of the natural sciences, and it was the model used in the early prescriptions for strategic planning." Of course, this entirely begs the question. Thus, Ansoff fails to address Mintzberg's Hayekian challenge.

Strategy process research remains a relatively small area. Partly, this may be because it lacks a clear underpinning. Most strategy research remains based, one way or the other, on some mainstream economic model. As the Austrians have always emphasized, such models are timeless equilibrium models that do not explicitly treat process. Strategy research based on such foundations does easily align with process issues. This is one reason why we have argued that our entrepreneurial perspective is a natural complement to resource-based approaches; that is, an entrepreneurial perspective informed by the judgment-based view laid out in Sections 3 and 4 provides insight into the creation of competitive advantages. However, the Hayekian perspective on the nature of knowledge for decision-making and how such knowledge is dispersed in social systems also provides insights into strategy processes because it highlights the difficulties of identifying and integrating such knowledge, and because it high-lights the fleeting, subjective and tacit nature of knowledge as a potential source of advantage. As we shall see in the following section, these Hayekian points also have implications for our understanding of firm organization.

Conclusions

Since its beginnings as an academic field in the 1970s, the field of strategy has evolved and expanded considerably. To take only one example, in the main professional association for management scholars, the Academy of Management, the strategy division is now the largest. Along with entrepreneur-ship, strategy is the field of management most directly related to Austrian economics, and also the one that has most explicitly made use of Austrian ideas. However, as we have indicated, strategy could make much more use of Austrian insights. Thus, while strategy's dominant view, the RBV, possess some key similarities to Austrian work, it lacks a unifying underpinning of its key ideas. Where is "resource heterogeneity," really? Why is it that firms that acquire resources on strategic factor markets may value these resources differently? Why do some strategy processes succeed and others fail? Austrian research can inform such key questions, which currently lack strong answers, in important ways.

6 The Entrepreneurial Nature of the Firm

Introduction

Following Coase's seminal 1937 article, "The Nature of the Firm," and later foundational contributions from Alchian and Demsetz (1972), Williamson (1975, 1985), Jensen and Meckling (1976), Hart (1995), and others, the economic analysis of the firm has become an increasingly important part of management research. And yet, while the firm is primarily an entrepreneurial endeavor – firms are established and maintained by entrepreneurs, and entrepreneurship is typically manifested in the creation, dissolution, and restructuring of firms – the links between entrepreneurship theory and the theory of the firm are only recently beginning to be explored. While much of the early modern entrepreneurship literature focused on individuals (Cooper & Dunkelberg, 1986; Hisrich & Brush, 1987; Gartner, 1988; Evans & Jovanovic, 1989) or on highly abstract conceptions of the entrepreneurial function, the contemporary literature is increasingly interested in tying entrepreneurship to strategy and organization.[27]

Austrian economics can help bridge this gap. Within most approaches in economics the entrepreneur is treated as an afterthought or ignored completely, or entrepreneurship is understood as a special topic such as new-venture creation or firm growth. In contrast, entrepreneurship has always played a central role in the Austrian understanding of markets, as noted in Sections 2 and 3. Austrian insights have much to say about the nature and organization of the firm and the role entrepreneurs play in creating and maintaining business organizations. Hence, an Austrian approach to the firm – its nature, origins, boundaries, and internal structure – has a uniquely entrepreneurial flavor.

Entrepreneurship, Production, and Capital

As noted in Section 2, one of the Austrian school's distinct contributions is its approach to capital and production, which emphasizes the complexity and heterogeneity of capital goods, the time structure of production, and the role of the entrepreneur in appraising the value of capital goods in alternative uses.

---

[27] The establishment of the *Strategic Entrepreneurship Journal* in 2006 is an example of the broadening of entrepreneurship beyond the individual level.

Klein (1996) points out that Mises's famous argument about the impossibility of economic calculation under socialism is not really about socialism per se, but the need for market prices for intermediate goods used in production. It is essentially a statement about the value of cost accounting. Mises argued that, due to the nearly infinite number of potential combinations of capital and other inputs available in a market economy, entrepreneurs cannot determine the least costly (and hence most profitable) use of inputs to produce particular outputs without meaningful prices for all inputs (cf. also Section 5). Choosing the combinations with the least weight or volume, or using the least amount of labor, or occupying the smallest parcel of land, makes no sense given the heterogeneity of inputs and the wide variation in their economic values. Socialism cannot allocate resources efficiently because the state owns the means of production and hence there are no markets for factors of production, no factor prices, and no means of comparing the economic cost or value of alternative input combinations.

In other words, a market economy is essentially an entrepreneurial one in which entrepreneurs use economic calculation to assemble, configure, and recombine bundles of heterogeneous resources to produce goods and services that can be sold to consumers for a profit (Foss et al., 2007). The role of entrepreneurs in production is the context for Mises's (1949: 248) oft-cited quote about their importance:

> [I]t is impossible to eliminate the entrepreneur from the picture of a market economy. The various complementary factors of production cannot come together spontaneously. They need to be combined by the purposive efforts of men aiming at certain ends and motivated by the urge to improve their state of satisfaction. In eliminating the entrepreneur one eliminates the driving force of the whole market system.

Friedrich von Wieser was the first to develop a theory of factor pricing based on the marginal contribution of inputs to the value of outputs, which came to be called the theory of *imputation*. Unlike the classical economists (including Marx), who thought the value of goods and services depended on the value of the inputs used to produce them (particularly labor), the Austrians argued that the causal relationship went in the other direction: the value of inputs (including labor) is "imputed" from the value to consumers of the goods and services they produce, given particular production plans guided by entrepreneurs. In a long-run equilibrium, factor prices will equal their discounted marginal revenue products, leaving no surplus or residual for the entrepreneur. Under uncertainty, however, entrepreneurs bid for factors based on their estimates of marginal revenue products that will only be realized later, once final goods have been produced and sold. Entrepreneurs with superior judgment can obtain factors at prices below their eventually realized values, generating profits, while those who judge the future incorrectly will pay too much, resulting in losses. Competition, in this view, is the continual process of entrepreneurs "testing" their judgments about future prices (and other aspects of production) against the reality of the market.

The Organization of Production

Until the 1970s, the "theory of the firm" mainly referred to production theory. This was particularly true of neoclassical economics, despite the popularity of Coase's pioneering 1937 article which directed economists' attention to the nature and inner workings of the business firm as an organization. The works by Williamson, Alchian, Demsetz, and others mentioned earlier built upon Coase to develop a theory of firm boundaries and internal structure. But the Austrians were also slow to develop a theory of the firm-as-organization, despite developing other important insights into incentives, information, and governance (Mises, 1944; Foss, 1994; Klein, 1996).

The lack of a distinct Austrian theory of the firm is surprising because the Hayekian notion of dispersed, tacit knowledge, and the need for rules and institutions such as the price mechanism to help agents navigate a world of tacit knowledge, is fundamental to organization theory. The "knowledge-based view" of the firm (Nonaka & Takeuchi, 1995; Grant, 1996) sees tacit knowledge as the firm's main asset and potential source of competitive advantage and focuses on how organizations develop, govern, and exploit knowledge resources. Jensen and Meckling's (1992) influential distinction between "specific" and "general" knowledge is strongly influenced by Hayek. They develop a theory of delegation based on the idea that when valuable knowledge is costly to transfer, organizations should assign decision authority to agents who already possess the necessary knowledge – echoing Hayek's idea that a market economy delegates decision authority to the "man on the spot" (Hayek, 1945: 524) who has the knowledge of local circumstances.[28]

Contrary to some modern perspectives on organizations in today's "knowledge-based" society, however, Austrian economics suggests a continuing role for the managerial hierarchy. Key to the Austrian approach to the firm is the notion of ownership as ultimate decision authority about the use of productive resources under uncertainty (Foss & Klein, 2012). (This view of ownership is also found in Knight, 1921, as well as contemporary property-rights approaches to the firm.)

---

[28] See Foss and Klein (2014) for a detailed discussion of Hayek's influence on organization studies.

In other words, the market makes use of tacit, dispersed knowledge, as argued by Hayek, but it does so mainly within firms, famously described as "islands of conscious power" (Robertson, 1923: quoted in Coase, 1937: 338) within the sea of the market economy.[29]

Why do firms exist? Coase (1937) argued that entrepreneurs establish firms to mitigate the transaction costs of coordinating production via the price mechanism. Inside the firm, the entrepreneur coordinates by fiat, which, under certain circumstances, allows for a more effective division of labor for highly interdependent tasks (Bylund, 2011, 2015). Foss and Klein (2012) offer a different explanation: entrepreneurs establish firms to overcome what Knight (1921) described as the non-contractibility of entrepreneurial judgment. Because the entrepreneur cannot articulate her beliefs about future prices and market conditions, her confidence in the viability of her business plan, and other elements of her idiosyncratic judgment, she must take ownership of complementary capital goods to put her beliefs into practice. Under uncertainty, entrepreneurial action implies "ultimate responsibility which in its very nature cannot be insured nor capitalized nor salaried" (Knight, 1921: 310).

Firm boundaries, then, are determined by the relative advantages of internal coordination under the control of an entrepreneur-owner and external coordination via markets and prices (after all, the firm is competing against other firms). While this approach is generally consistent with Coase's, it offers a different definition of what a firm "is." Coase (1937) identifies the firm in terms of the employment relation. A one-person operation, in this definition, is not a firm, and vertical integration deals with the question of adding producers of intermediate products to the firm's employment roll. For Knight, Williamson, and Hart, by contrast, the firm is defined not by the employment relationship, but by the ownership of alienable assets. In this approach, the question is who owns what, not who is employed by whom.

Austrians have explained vertical integration in terms of asset specificity and incomplete contracting, as in transaction cost (Williamson, 1985) and property-rights (Hart, 1990) approaches, as well as the industry life-cycle (Langlois, 2003). However, Austrian economics offers unique insights on the limits to the firm, a somewhat ambiguous issue in transaction cost economics. In general, the limits to firm size can be understood as a special case of Mises's (1920) and Hayek's (1937, 1945) arguments about the impossibility of rational economic planning under socialism. Kirzner (1992: 162), for instance, uses Hayekian language: "In a free market, any advantages that may be derived from 'central

---

[29] Hayek's distinction between "spontaneous" and "planned" orders closely parallels that between "markets and hierarchies" (Williamson, 1975), or "spontaneous" and "intentional" governance (Williamson, 1991).

planning' ... are purchased at the price of an enhanced knowledge problem. We may expect firms to spontaneously expand to the point where additional advantages of 'central planning' are just offset by the incremental knowledge difficulties that stem from dispersed information." Rothbard (1962: 544–50) focuses on Mises's argument, claiming that the need for monetary calculation in terms of actual prices not only explains the failures of central planning under socialism, but places an upper bound on firm size.

Mises had argued that factors can only be allocated to their highest-valued uses when their marginal values are revealed in competitive factor markets. Without private ownership and market prices, socialist planners cannot know the actual opportunity costs of resources and can only make educated guesses about efficient resource allocation. Rothbard pointed out that the same argument applies also to the private entrepreneur. For example, if the entrepreneur's capabilities are completely specific to the firm, she cannot estimate the implicit cost of her foregone outside earnings and cannot calculate the actual profitability of her venture. Likewise, a vertically integrated firm needs market-based transfer prices for all internally transferred goods and services to calculate the profitability of its subunits. If the firm becomes so large that it is the sole buyer and seller of an intermediate good, or its internally transferred goods are so specialized that there are no outside buyers or sellers, then the firm faces the same "calculation problem" as the centrally planned economy.

Authority and Delegation

Given the Austrian school's emphasis on private property and decentralized decision-making, one might expect "Austrian" treatments of the firm to highlight the benefits of delegation, worker empowerment, flexibility, and flatter hierarchies. Indeed, Cowen and Parker (1997) take this line:

> Market changes are moving manufacturing farther and farther away from steady-state, low variety, long-batch production runs, relevant to Taylorist methods, to high variety and small runs ... Organizations are adopting new forms of decentralization to cope with the instability, uncertainty, and pace of change of the marketplace ... In cluster of network working, employees of undifferentiated rank may operate temporarily on a certain task or tasks in teams. The clusters are largely autonomous and engage in decentralized decision-making and planning ... They are conducive to individual initiative ("intrapreneurship") and faster decision-taking. They facilitate organizational flexibility.

Similar accounts can be found in popular management writings by Peters (1994), Tapscott and Williams (2006), Kastelle (2013), and many others.

However, the empirical evidence on the flattening hierarchy is, well, flat. During the last few decades many firms have increased their use of performance-based pay, work teams, and other forms of delegation (Milgrom & Roberts, 1995; Ichniowski, Shaw, & Prennushi, 1997; Bresnahan, Brynjolfsson, & Hitt, 2002). There is some evidence for reduced layers of management in US corporations (e.g., Rajan & Wulf, 2006). Yet it is difficult to discern an overall trend toward eliminating the managerial hierarchy or in treating firms and markets, as "different means of organizing economic activity ... that do not differ substantially in kind" (Cowen and Parker, 1997:15).

Foss and Klein (2014) offer an alternative interpretation of the role of authority and delegation in the "knowledge economy." As they point out, authority can mean either commanding subordinates to perform specific tasks (what Simon, 1951, calls "Type I authority"), or designing incentive schemes, monitoring systems, means of resolving disputes, and other mechanisms ("Type II authority"). What we have seen in recent years is decreased use of the former type and increased use of the latter. Consider, for example, the popular contrast between a traditional, hierarchically produced encyclopedia and the online, open-source, collaborative project Wikipedia. A crowdsourced encyclopedia seems like a prototypical example of Hayekian spontaneous order (and Wikipedia founder Jimmy Wales has cited Hayek as an inspiration). But Wikipedia is, in a fundamental sense, designed: the software that manages the structure, display, editing protocols, and dispute resolution procedures, is not itself the product of spontaneous order, but was created by the designers of Wikipedia. Likewise, even highly decentralized companies like Zappos and Valve have owners and managers responsible for hiring and firing employees, designing tasks, evaluating performance, and bearing the "ultimate responsibility" for managing the firm's tangible assets under conditions of Knightian uncertainty (e.g. Foss & Dobrajska, 2015). The death of the managerial hierarchy, Foss and Klein (2014) maintain, has been greatly exaggerated.

Put differently, there is a role for "Coasean authority in Hayekian settings" (Foss, 2001). Under uncertainty, ownership conveys authority, even if owners choose to delegate a substantial amount of day-to-day discretion to subordinates. Decision-rights are delegated as means to an end (Hayek 1973), their use is monitored (Jensen and Meckling 1992), and top-management reserves ultimate decision-rights for itself (Baker, Gibbons, and Murphy 1999). Foss, Foss, and Klein (2007) develop a theory of delegation in which owners exercise "original judgment" and subordinates with substantial decision-authority exercise "derived judgment"; that is, they are tasked with acting as if they were owners, on behalf of the actual owners they serve. The entrepreneur-owner must then balance the benefits of assigning decision authority to employees possessing valuable tacit knowledge against the potential harms from agents using their discretion to pursue their own goals at the expense of the firm's.

The result is what Foss, Foss, and Klein (2007) call a "nested hierarchy of judgment." Lachmann expresses a similar notion of delegation, using the terms "capitalist-entrepreneur" and "manager-entrepreneur" to describe those exercising original and derived judgment, respectively. The key for Lachmann is the hierarchy of "specification" in which the capitalist-entrepreneur establishes the conditions under which the manager-operator acts, and so on down the line (Lachmann 1956: 98–99).

> For the sake of terminological clarity it is desirable to call an "entrepreneur" anybody who is concerned with the management of assets ... [A]s regards capital, the function of the entrepreneur consists in specifying and modifying the concrete form of the capital resources committed to his care.
>
> We might then distinguish between the capitalist-entrepreneur and the manager-entrepreneur. The only significant difference between the two lies in that the specifying and modifying decisions of the manager presuppose and are consequent upon the decisions of the capitalist. If we like, we may say that the latter's decisions are of a "higher order."
>
> Thus a capitalist makes a first specifying decision by deciding to invest a certain amount of capital, which probably, though not necessarily, exists in the money form, in Company A rather than in Company B, or rather than to lend it to the government. The managers of Company A then make a second specifying decision by deciding to use the capital so received in building or extending a department store in one suburb rather than another suburb, or another city. The manager of this local department store makes further specifying decisions, and so on, until the capital has been converted into concrete assets.

These "specifying decisions" are the formal and implicit contracts by which the entrepreneur delegates judgment to subordinates in the multi-person organization. The entrepreneur, by virtue of owning alienable assets under uncertainty, decides what decision-rights and responsibilities non-owner employees will hold, leading to a hierarchical nesting of decision authority. Thus, firms may exercise a high degree of delegation without ceasing to be firms, to be "organizations" rather than "orders" in Hayek's sense.

Austrian economics also goes beyond agency theory in suggesting that ownership of assets is itself a sort of capability which differs among individuals, thus determining in a competitive market the assignment of roles to principal and agent (Foss, Foss, & Klein, 2007; Topan, 2012; Foss & Klein, 2018). Those individuals with greater capabilities at exercising the ownership function will tend to accumulate resources and to exercise entrepreneurial judgment to a greater extent. Rather than assigning residual decision-making authority to non-owner stakeholders, firms are generally better off letting equity holders exercise "primary judgment," while delegating other rights and responsibilities to workers, suppliers, and other participants in the web of contracts and relationships that constitute the firm's activities.

Conclusions

Austrian economics thus offers unique insights into the canonical "Coasean" questions of the existence, boundaries, and internal organization of the firm. Entrepreneurs establish firms as mechanisms for exploiting their tacit and idiosyncratic judgments about the uncertain future as they transform heterogeneous capital resources into future consumer goods and services. The firm's strategy and structure emerge endogenously and experimentally as entrepreneurs subject their judgments to the reality of market competition. Unlike the static, equilibrium models of the firm found in neoclassical economics, an entrepreneurial Austrian theory accounts for innovation, testing and revision of business plans, and other features familiar to practitioners. And, contrary to casual observations about liberty and spontaneous order, Austrian economics associates ownership with responsibility, which is typically manifested in some form of managerial hierarchy.

7 The Future of Austrian Economics in Management Research

The Increasing Influence of Austrian Economics on Management Thought

Like most economists until recently, Austrian economists have often taken little interest in management research or practice. (However, a case could be made that Mises's book *Bureaucracy* is essentially an important contribution to early organization theory.) Partly, this reflects the fact that management research arrived on the scene much later than economics. Moreover, when management research began to thrive in the 1960s, the Austrian school was almost extinct. When it was revitalized in the 1970s, most of the younger Austrians chose to work on traditional Austrian topics (methodology, the economics of socialism, business-cycle theory, etc.) rather than on those parts of economics with a strong potential to inform management research, such as the economics of the firm and industrial organization more broadly. In hindsight, this was a missed opportunity.

And yet, Austrian economics deals with *fundamental* issues common to all social sciences and management disciplines – human beings acting in the presence of scarcity and uncertainty, exercising judgment in order to improve their lots, and paying attention to the opportunity costs of alternative actions.

Austrian work seeks to examine not only people acting in isolation, but also interacting in various institutional and social settings. As such, it is highly valuable for framing business problems in a realistic manner, for example, by giving accounts of entrepreneurship or the "calculation problems" that can beset the internal organization of firms. Not surprisingly, there has been some use of Austrian ideas in management thought, as we have indicated throughout this Element. Indeed, the slowly but steadily increasing stream of publications that draw on Austrian ideas is a testament to their continuing value for both management research and economics.

Moreover, we think that macro-management theory has become much more *potentially* receptive to Austrian ideas over the last few decades, particularly in those areas already partly shaped by economics, that is, entrepreneurship, strategy, and organization (and derived fields, such as international business and technology strategy). The reasons are many, but have to do with a greater appreciation of heterogeneity at all levels (from individuals over organizations to nations); asymmetric and private information, including knowledge with "Austrian" properties (subjective, tacit, fleeting, etc.); not only risk and uncertainty, but also notions that individuals and organizations navigate the social landscape on the basis of personal beliefs and theories of that landscape; methodological individualism, known in management research as "microfoundations"; and other themes that are if not always uniquely associated with Austrian economics, are strongly connected with it.

Likewise, we think that advances on the level of modeling and empirical methods in some key ways pull in the direction of the Austrian school. Thus, the increased use of simulation models is one way in which some of the causal relations involved in the "market process" can be modeled and traced. While simulations certainly have limitations, they can partially address the characteristic Austrian critique of "process-less" models in social science. Thus, a simulation that sets out in a step-by-step manner exactly what goes on in an artificial social context over time (Nell, 2010). This method also helps to address the Austrian method of explaining social outcomes, such as institutions, in terms of causal mechanisms that have plausibly produced the relevant outcome (i.e., "conjectural history").

On the level of empirical methods, the recent push toward more explicit "identification" of the real causes of observed events, while not Austrian-inspired, is something Austrians are likely to applaud. Although they may criticize the lack of explicit attention to causal *mechanisms* in much recent work on econometric identification, Austrians can certainly support the increased attention to causal relationships over simultaneous determination represented by the current "credibility revolution." Similarly, the shift in mainstream economics toward applied microeconomics and the current emphasis on microdata (i.e., the use of large-scale register datasets on individual-level characteristics) is a welcome improvement, from the perspective of methodological individualism, over the 1950s–1980s primacy of highly aggregate, a-theoretical macroeconomic models, even if much current micro-level analysis abstracts from actual behavior. In the domain of "small-N" (i.e., qualitative, or "case" research), many improvements have also occurred over the last few decades, allowing management scholars to provide accounts of "how it really happened" that are both fine-grained and rigorous.

Other Fields in Business and Management

We have concentrated on how the Austrian approach to economics can extend current work in entrepreneurship, strategy, and organization studies. However, Austrian ideas also apply to other fields in business and management. For example, Mises's analysis of economic calculation, as explained above, is essentially about cost accounting. The role of property and prices in guiding managerial decisions helps explain the rise of newer approaches such as activity-based costing (Taylor, 2000) and the use of market-based transfer prices (Staubus, 1986). The Austrian understanding of marginalism is reflected in the concept of economic value added (Stern, Stewart, & Chew, 1995). And of course, the notion of opportunity cost, fundamental to all theories of intra-firm resource allocation, was initially developed and expounded by the Austrian economists.

In marketing, Ekelund and Saurman (1988), Hunt and Morgan (1995), and Hunt (2000) build on Austrian notions of competition to develop insights for marketing theory and practice. If competition is, as Hayek (1968) called it, a "discovery procedure," then entrepreneurs benefit not only from (passive) acts of price discovery, but also from (active) attempts to disseminate price information to consumers through advertising. An Austrian perspective on competition cuts through old debates about whether advertising and other marketing activities are "pro-" or "anti-competitive." These debates typically have the neoclassical notion of perfect competition in mind as their performance benchmark. Once we recognize that competition is a dynamic, rivalrous process of interaction among firms, each trying to outperform its rivals, the distinction melts away: "All activities that contribute to positions of competitive advantage or the absence of which would contribute to positions of competitive disadvantage are presumptively pro-competitive – marketing activities are no exception to this rule" (Hunt & Morgan, 1995: 10).

In finance, ideas from Austrian theories of money, banking, and financial markets have been influential in investment theory, particularly the notion of "value investing" (Calandro, 2004, 2009 Grimm, 2012; Spitznagel, 2013). And while business-cycle theory is usually considered outside the domain of management studies, there are important parallels (as noted in previous sections) between Austrian capital theory and concepts of resource heterogeneity from transaction cost economics and the RBV of the firm (Agarwal et al., 2009). The Austrian theory of the business cycle has enjoyed a renaissance since the global financial crisis of 2008, which mainstream macroeconomics was ill-equipped to anticipate or remedy. In the wake of the crisis it became particularly clear that many economists had failed to look realistically at the way entrepreneurs behaved in the boom period, and how their decisions affected the severity of the bust. In response, a new literature has emerged that focuses on using Austrian ideas to explain entrepreneurs' decision processes during the businesses cycle (e.g. Engelhardt, 2012).

A more straightforward application of Austrian entrepreneurship theory is the problem of entrepreneurial finance. If entrepreneurial judgment under uncertainty is sufficiently tacit and idiosyncratic that entrepreneurs cannot convince outside parties to invest – the central idea behind Knight's (1921) theory of the firm – then we would expect to see new ventures financed exclusively through bootstrapping or debt. However, investments from business angels and venture capitalists are increasingly important in modern economies. Foss, Klein, and Murtinu (2018) address this seeming paradox by pointing out that new-venture funding represents investment both in projects (resources with salvage values) and in entrepreneurs (tacit, subjective judgments and capabilities). Angels and venture capitalists, as well as individuals who start new companies, are exercising a measure of entrepreneurial judgment, in judging potential founders. These founders face a trade-off between choosing resources that are more closely complementary to their own idiosyncratic judgments – so that outside equity investors are betting purely on the entrepreneur – and choosing resources that are less specific, so the investor has more protection against failure of the venture.

We have emphasized throughout this Element that Austrian economics strives for realism and practicality. It should not come as a surprise then that it has a role to play in business history as well as theory. Austrians can and should contribute to the "historical turn" in management studies, and in some sense, they already are. For example, leading historians of entrepreneurship like Mark Casson often rely on Austrian ideas to interpret historical cases (e.g. Casson & Casson, 2013). To take a specific example of one path this research might take, there is room for exploring how institutions have historically influenced entrepreneurial decision-making and helped steer societies toward or away from productive market entrepreneurship (McCaffrey, 2017; Bylund & McCaffrey, 2017).

Austrians ideas are being applied in research on firms within commercial society, yet they also have potential for use in management and organization studies outside the traditional marketplace. This is especially true of theories of entrepreneurship and economic calculation. One place where these concepts can be especially useful is in the area of conflict studies, for example, research on military organization. This field often struggles with classic questions from economics and management relating to problems like the size and shape of military organizations, their internal incentive compatibility and efficient use of scarce resources, the uncertainty and incomplete information facing their leaders, and so on (McCaffrey, 2014b, 2015b). These and other topics can be analyzed in light of Austrian contributions. The most crucial of these is the idea that the profit and loss test of the market, along with the use of money prices to allocate scarce resources, provides an indispensable framework for decision-making that does not exist in the military sphere. Military organizers therefore confront similar limitations as bureaucrats attempting to centrally plan a national economy.

Conclusions

Management research is constituted by a set of highly diverse and fragmented fields. Part of the reason is the fact that management, in the context of science and research in general, is a recent undertaking. It also reflects the fact that management draws eclectically on multiple disciplines and fields, ranging from mathematics and biology to the social sciences to law and the humanities. It is hard to see what unites operations research, strategy, and organizational behavior research. This makes management siloed and at best cumulative within discipline-specific silos. In fact, even the management fields themselves are seriously fragmented. For example, organization theory includes both the highly formal economics-based theory of principals and agents alongside currents such as sociological-institutional theory. Again, it is hard to discern any overlap except a shared concern with organized human activity.

Perhaps the strongest overall case for Austrian economics playing a useful role in management research is that it is sufficiently flexible to speak to and inform multiple management fields. Indeed, the Austrian school is beginning to be recognized as a rich, diverse, and evolving body of literature, not a fixed set of theories or conclusions on a narrow set of issues. What is assumed about human behavior in various strands of Austrian work is not directly at variance with much research in organizational behavior (the mainstream economic model of expected utility maximization basically is). Austrian economics relates both to economic approaches to organization and to more psychological and sociologically informed views that emphasize the cognitive and institutional dimensions of organizations. Austrian research has direct and powerful implications for entrepreneurship and strategy. We could continue to make this case through examples, but we believe we have established that few other social science approaches have a similar integrative potential. In other words – although this would perhaps have been very surprising to the original Austrians – Austrian economics is to a large extent the language of management research.

References

Abell, Peter, Teppo Felin, and Nicolai Foss. 2008. "Building MicroFoundations for the Routines, Capabilities, and Performance Links." *Managerial and Decision Economics*. 29: 489–502.

Abu-Saifan, Samer. 2012. "Social Entrepreneurship: Definitions and Boundaries."*Technology Innovation Management Review*. 2 (2): 22–27.

Acs, Zoltan and David B. Audretsch. 1990. *Innovation and Small Firms*. Cambridge, MA: MIT Press.

Agafonow, A. 2015. "Value Creation, Value Capture, and Value Devolution: Where Do Social Enterprises Stand?" *Administration & Society*. 47(8): 1038–60.

Agarwal, Rajshree, Jay B. Barney, Nicolai Foss, and Peter G. Klein. 2009. "Heterogeneous Resources and the Financial Crisis: Implications of Strategic Management Theory," *Strategic Organization*. 7(4): 467–84.

Alchian, Armen A., and Harold Demsetz. 1972. "Production, Information Costs, and Economic Organization." *American Economic Review*. 62(5): 777–95.

Aldrich, Howard E. 1990. "Using an Ecological Perspective to Study Organizational Founding Rates." *Entrepreneurship Theory and Practice*. 14 (3): 7–24.

Alvord, Sarah H., L. David Brown, and Christine W. Letts. 2004. "Social Entrepreneurship and Societal Transformation an Exploratory Study." *Journal of Applied Behavioral Science*. 40 (3): 260–82.

Andrade, Gregor, Mark Mitchell, and Erik Stafford. 2001. "New Evidence and Perspectives on Mergers." *Journal of Economic Perspectives*. 15: 103–20.

Ansoff, H. Igor. 1965. *Corporate strategy: An analytic approach to business policy for growth and expansion*. McGraw-Hill Companies.

Ansoff, H. I. 1991. Critique of Henry Mintzberg's 'The design school: reconsidering the basic premises of strategic management'. *Strategic management Journal*. 12 (6): 449–461.

Ardichvili, Alexander, Richard Cardozo, and Souray Ray. 2003. "A Theory of Entrepreneurial Opportunity Identification and Development." *Journal of Business Venturing*. 18(1): 105–23.

Audretsch, David B., Max Keilbach, and Erik Lehmann. 2005. *Entrepreneurship and Economic Growth*. Oxford University Press.

Baker, George, Robert Gibbons, and Kevin J. Murphy. 1999. "Informal Authority in Organizations." *Journal of Law, Economics, and Organization*. 15 (1): 56.

Bain, J. S. 1956. *Barriers to New Competition*, Cambridge, MA: Harvard University Press.

Barney, Jay B. 1986. "Organizational Culture: Can It Be a Source of Sustained Competitive Advantage?" *Academy of Management Review.* 11(3): 656–65.

Barney, Jay B. 1991. "Firm Resources and Sustained Competitive Advantage." *Journal of Management.* 17: 99–120.

Baron, R.A., and Ensley, M.D. 2006. "Opportunity Recognition as the Detection of Meaningful Patterns: Evidence from Comparisons of Novice and Experienced Entrepreneurs." *Management Science.* 52 (9): 1331–1344.

Baumol, William J. 1990. "Entrepreneurship: Productive, Unproductive, and Destructive." *Journal of Political Economy.* 98(5): 893–921.

Bewley, Truman F. 1986. "Knightian Decision Theory: Part I." *Cowles Foundation Discussion Paper No. 807.*

Bewley, Truman F. 1989. "Market Innovation and Entrepreneurship: A Knightian View." *Cowles Foundation Discussion Paper No. 905.*

Black, Janice A. and Kimberly E. Boal. 1994. "Strategic Resources: Traits, Configurations and Paths to Sustainable Competitive Advantage." *Strategic Management Journal.* 15: 131–148.

Bloom, P. N. 2012. "Introduction to the Special Section on Social Entrepreneurship." *Journal of Public Policy & Marketing.* 31(1): 73–74.

Böhm-Bawerk, E. von. 1959. *Positive Theory of Capital.* Trans. George D. Huncke and Hans F. Sennholz. South Holland, IL: Libertarian Press.

Böhm-Bawerk, E. von. 1962. "The Austrian Economists." In *Shorter Classics of Böhm-Bawerk.* South Holland, IL: Libertarian Press, pp. 1–24.

Boot, Arnoud W. A., Todd T. Milbourn, and Anjan V. Thakor . 1999. "Megamergers and Expanded Scope: Theories of Bank Size and Activity Diversity." *Journal of Banking and Finance.* 23: 195–214.

Bresnahan, Timothy F., Erik Brynjolfsson, and Lorin M. Hitt. 2002. "Information Technology, Workplace Organization, and the Demand for Skilled Labor: Firm-Level Evidence." *Quarterly Journal of Economics.* 117 (1): 339–376.

Buchanan, J. M. 1969. *Cost and Choice: An Inquiry in Economic Theory.* Chicago: University of Chicago Press.

Bylund, Per L. 2011. "Division of Labor and the Firm: An Austrian Attempt at Explaining the Firm in the Market." *Quarterly Journal of Austrian Economics.* 14 (2): 188–215.

Bylund, P.L., 2015. *The Problem of Production: A new theory of the firm.* New York: Routledge.

Bylund, P. L. and McCaffrey, M. 2017. "A Theory of Entrepreneurship and Institutional Uncertainty." *Journal of Business Venturing.* 32 (5), 461–75.

Calandro, Joseph. 2004. "Reflexivity, Business Cycles, and the new Economy." *Quarterly Journal of Austrian Economics*. 7(3): 45–69.

Calandro, Joseph. 2009. *Applied Value Investing*. New York: McGraw-Hill.

Casson, Mark C. 1982. *The Entrepreneur: An Economic Theory*. Second edition, Aldershot, U.K.: Edward Elgar, 1999.

Casson, M. & Casson, C. 2013. *The Entrepreneur in History: From Medieval Merchant to Modern Business Leader*. Basingstoke: Palgrave Macmillan.

Coase, Ronald H. 1937. "The Nature of the Firm." *Economica*. 4: 386–405.

Cooper, A. C. and Dunkelberg, W. C. 1986, "Entrepreneurship and Paths to Business Ownership." *Strategic Management Journal*. 7: 53–68.

Cowen, Tyler and David Parker. 1997. *Markets in the Firm: A Market-Process Approach to Management*. London: Institute of Economic Affairs.

Cyert, Richard M., and James G. March. 1963. *A Behavioral Theory of the Firm*. Englewood Cliffs, N.J.: Prentice-Hall.

Dacin, P. A., Dacin, M. T. and M. Matear. 2010. "Social Entrepreneurship: Why We Don't Need a New Theory and How We Move Forward From Here." *Academy of Management Perspectives*. 24 (3): 37–57.

Davidson, A.B. and Ekelund Jr, R.B., 1994. "Can Entrepreneurship Be 'Unproductive?' Towards An Evolutionary Interpretation." *Review of Social Economy*. 52(4), 266–79.

Debreu, Gerard. 1959. *Theory of Value*. New York: Wiley.

Dees, J. Gregory. 1998. "Enterprising Nonprofits." *Harvard Business Review*. 76: 54–67.

Demsetz, Harold. 1972. "When does the rule of liability matter?" *The Journal of Legal Studies*. 1(1): 13–28.

Demsetz, H. 1973. Industry Structure, Market Rivalry and Public Policy. *Journal of Law and Economics*. 16: 1–9.

Demsetz, Harold. 1983. "The structure of ownership and the theory of the firm." *The Journal of Law and Economics*. 26(2): 375–90.

Denrell, Jerker., C. Fang, and Sidney G. Winter. 2003. "The Economics of Strategic Opportunity." *Strategic Management Journal*. 24(10): 977–90.

Dierickx, Ingemar, and Karel Cool. 1989. "Asset Stock Accumulation and Sustainability of Competitive Advantage." *Management Science*. 35: 1504–11.

Dimov, D., 2007. Beyond the single-person, single-insight attribution in understanding entrepreneurial opportunities. *Entrepreneurship Theory and Practice*. 31(5), pp.713–731.

Dorobat, C.E. and Topan, M.V., 2015. "Entrepreneurship and comparative advantage." *Journal of Entrepreneurship*. 24(1), 1–16.

Douhan, R. and Henrekson, M. 2010. "Entrepreneurship and Second-Best Institutions: Going Beyond Baumol's Typology." *Journal of Evolutionary Economics*. 20 (4), 629–643.

Easterby-Smith, Mark, and Lyles, Marjorie. 2011. *Handbook of Organizational Learning and Knowledge Management*. 2nd ed., New York: Wiley.

Emerson, Jed, and Fay Twersky (eds.). 1996. *New Social Entrepreneurs: The Success, Challenge and Lessons of Non-Profit Enterprise Creation*. San Francisco: The Roberts Foundation.

Engelhardt, Lucas. 2012. "Expansionary Monetary Policy and Decreasing Entrepreneurial Quality." *Quarterly Journal of Austrian Economics*. 15 (2), 172–194.

Ekelund, Robert.B., and Saurman, David S. 1988 *Advertising and the Market Process: A Modern Economic View*. San Francisco: Pacific Research Institute For Public Policy.

Evans, David S., and Boyan Jovanovic. 1989. "An Estimated Model of Entrepreneurial Choice under Liquidity Constraints." *Journal of Political Economy*. 97(4): 808–827.

Felin, Teppo, and Nicolai J. Foss. 2005. "Strategic Organization: A Field in Search of Micro-Foundations." *Strategic Organization*. 3(4): 441–55.

Fetter, Frank A. 1915. *Economic Principles*. New York: The Century Co.

Fetter, Frank A. 1936. 'Cost-Prices, Product-Prices, and Profits.' In *Economic Principles and Problems: Volume I*, 3rd edition, ed. Walter E. Spahr. New York: Farrar and Rinehart.

Foss, Kirsten. 2001. "Organizing Technological Interdependencies: A Coordination Perspective on the Firm." *Industrial and Corporate Change*. 10(1): 151–78.

Foss, Nicolai J. 2000. "Equilibrium versus Evolution: The Conflicting Legacies of Demsetz and Penrose." In N. J. Foss and P. Robertson. *Resources, Technology, and Strategy: Explorations in the Resource-based View*. London: Routledge.

Foss, Nicolai J. 2001. "Leadership, Beliefs and Coordination." *Industrial and Corporate Change*. 10: 357–388.

Foss, N. J. 1994. The theory of the firm: The Austrians as precursors and critics of contemporary theory. *The Review of Austrian Economics*. 7 (1), 31-65.

Foss, Nicolai J. 2005. *Strategy and Economic Organization in the Knowledge Economy: The Coordination of Firms and Resources*, Oxford: Oxford University Press.

Foss, Nicolai J., and Giampaolo Garzarelli, 2007. "Institutions as Knowledge Capital: Ludwig M. Lachmann's Interpretative Institutionalism." *Cambridge Journal of Economics*. 31(5): 789–804.

Foss, N.J. and Klein, P.G. 2012. *Organizing Entrepreneurial Judgment: A New Approach to the Firm.* Cambridge: Cambridge University Press

Foss, Nicolai J. and Snejina, Michailova. 2009. *Knowledge Governance: Processes and Perspectives.* New York: Oxford University Press.

Foss, Nicolai J., and Peter G. Klein. 2010. "Alertness, Action, and the Antecedents of Entrepreneurship." *Journal of Private Enterprise.* 25: 145–64.

Foss, Nicolai J., and Nils Stieglitz. 2011. "Modern Resource-based Theory." In M. Dietrich and J. Krafft, eds. *Handbook of the Economics of the Firm.* Edward Elgar.

Foss, Nicolai J., and Peter G. Klein. 2014. "Hayek and Organizational Studies," in Paul Adler, Paul du Gay, Glenn Morgan, and Mike Reed, eds., *Oxford Handbook of Sociology, Social Theory and Organization Studies: Contemporary Currents* (Oxford: Oxford University Press), pp. 467–86.

Foss, N.J. and Dobrajska, M., 2015. Valve's Way: Vayward, Visionary, or Voguish? *Journal of Organization Design.* 4(2), pp.12–15.

Foss, Nicolai J., and Peter G. Klein. 2018. "Stakeholders and Corporate Social Responsibility: An Ownership Perspective," in Sinziana Dorobantu, Ruth Aguilera, Jiao Luo, and Frances Milliken, eds., *Sustainability, Stakeholder Governance & Corporate Social Responsibility*, vol. 38 of *Advances in Strategic Management*, forthcoming.

Foss, N.J., and Klein, P.G. 2012. *Organizing Entrepreneurial Judgment: A New Approach to the Firm.* Cambridge: Cambridge University Press.

Foss, Nicolai J., Peter G. Klein, Samuele Murtinu. 2018. "Entrepreneurial finance under Knightian uncertainty." *Manuscript.*

Foss, Kirsten, Nicolai J. Foss, Peter G. Klein and Sandra Klein. 2007. "The Entrepreneurial Organization of Heterogeneous Capital." *Journal of Management Studies.* 44(7): 1165–186.

Foss, Nicolai J., Peter G. Klein, Yasemin Y. Kor, and Joseph T. Mahoney. 2008. "Entrepreneurship, Subjectivism, and the Resource-Based View: Towards a New Synthesis." *Strategic Entrepreneurship Journal.* 2(1): 73–94.

Foss, N.J. and Lyngsie, J. 2014. The strategic organization of the entrepreneurial established firm. *Strategic Organization*, 12(3): 208–215.

Friedman, M. and Savage, L.J. 1948. The utility analysis of choices involving risk. *Journal of Political Economy.* 56(4): 279–304.

Gaglio, C.M. and Katz J.A, 2001. "The Psychological Basis of Opportunity Identification: Entrepreneurial Alertness." *Small Business Economics.* 16: 95–111.

Galbraith, J.R. 1974. "Organization design: An information processing view." *Interfaces*. 4(3): 28-36.

Gartner, William B. 1988. "'Who Is an Entrepreneur?' Is the Wrong Question." *Entrepreneurship Theory and Practice*. 12(4): 11–32.

Gavetti, Giovanni and Daniel Levinthal. 2000. "Looking Forward and Looking Backward: Cognitive and Experiential Search." *Administrative Science Quarterly*. 45(1): 113–37.

Ghemawat, Pankaj. 2002. "Competition and business strategy in historical perspective." *Business History Review*. 76(1) 37–74.

Grant, Robert M. 1996. " Toward a Knowledge-Based Theory of the Firm." *Strategic Management Journal*. *17*: 109–122.

Grimm, Richard C. 2012. "Fundamental Analysis as a Traditional Austrian Approach to Common Stock Selection." *Quarterly Journal of Austrian Economics*. 15(2): 221–236.

Harding, R., 2004. "Social Enterprise: The New Economic Engine?" *Business Strategy Review*. 15 (4): 39–43.

Hart, Oliver D. 1995. *Firms, Contracts, and Financial Structure*. Oxford: The Clarendon Press.

Hart, Oliver D. 1990. "Is 'Bounded Rationality' an Important Element of a Theory of Institutions?" *Journal of Institutional and Theoretical Economics*. 16: 696–702.

Hastie, R. 2001. Problems for judgment and decision making. *Annual Review of Psychology*. *52*(1): 653–683.

Haugh, H. 2006. "Social Enterprise: Beyond Economic Outcomes and Individual Returns." In J. Mair, J. Robinson, and K. Hockerts (eds.), *Social Entrepreneurship*. Basingstoke, UK: Palgrave Macmillan, 180–205.

Hayek, F. A. 1937. "Economics and Knowledge." In idem. 1948. *Individualism and Economic Order*. Chicago: University of Chicago Press.

Hayek, F.A. 1941. *The Pure Theory of Capital*. London: Macmillan.

Hayek, F. A. 1945. "The Use of Knowledge in Society." In Hayek, 1948. *Individualism and Economic Order*. Chicago: Chicago University Press.

Hayek, Friedrich August. 1952. *The sensory order: An inquiry into the foundations of theoretical psychology*. University of Chicago Press.

Hayek, F.A. 1973 . *Law, Legislation and Liberty, volume I: Rules and Order*. Chicago: Chicago University Press.

Hayek, F.A. von. 1935. "The nature and history of the problem." In *Collectivist Economic Planning*, ed. F.A. Hayek. London: Routledge, pp. 1–40.

Henrekson, M. and Sanandaji, T. (2011). "The Interaction of Entrepreneurship and Institutions." *Journal of Institutional Economics*. 7 (1), 47–75.

Higgs, R., 1997. "Regime Uncertainty: Why the Great Depression Lasted So Long and Why Prosperity Resumed after the War." *Independent Review.* 1: 561–590.

Hisrich, Robert D., and Brush, Candida G. 1987. "Women Entrepreneurs: A Longitudinal Study." *Frontiers of Entrepreneurship Research.* 187(1): 566–578.

Huang, L., and J.L. Pearce., 2015, "Managing the Unknowable: The Effectiveness of Early-stage Investor Gut Feel in Entrepreneurial Investment Decisions." *Administrative Science Quarterly.* 60: 634–670.

Hunt, Shelby D. 2000. *A General Theory of Competition: Resources, Competences, Productivity, Economic Growth.* Thousand Oaks, Calif.: Sage.

Hunt, Shelby D., and Morgan, Robert M. 1995. "The Comparative Advantage Theory of Competition." *Journal of Marketing.* 59(2): 1–15.

Hutt, W.H. 1936. *Economists and the Public: A Study of Competition and Opinion.* London: Jonathan Cape.

Ichniowski, Casey, Kathryn Shaw, and G. Prennushi. 1997. "The Effects of Human Resource Management Practices on Productivity." *American Economic Review.* 87 (3): 291–313.

Jacobson, Robert. 1992. "The 'Austrian' School of Strategy." *Academy of Management Review.* 17: 782–807.

Jarrell, Gregg A., James A. Brickley, and Jeffry M. Netter. 1988. "The market for corporate control: the empirical evidence since 1980." *Journal of Economic Perspectives.* 2: 49–68.

Jensen, Michael C., and William H. Meckling. 1992. "Specific and General Knowledge, and Organizational Structure." In Lars Werin and Hans Wijkander, eds., *Contract Economics.*

Jensen, M. C., and Meckling, W. H. 1976. Theory of the firm: Managerial behavior, agency costs and ownership structure. *Journal of Financial Economics.* 3 (4), 305-360.

Kastelle, T., "Hierarchy is Overrated," *Harvard Business Review Blog,* November 30, 2013.

Kauffman, Stuart A. 1993. *The Origins of Order: Self-Organization and Section in Evolution.* New York: Oxford University Press.

Kihlstrom, Richard E., and Jean-Jacques Laffont. 1979. "A General Equilibrium Entrepreneurial Theory of Firm Formation Based on Risk Aversion." *Journal of Political Economy.* 87, no. 4: 719–748.

Kiessling, Timothy S. and R. Glenn Richey. 2004. "Examining the theoretical inspirations of a management guru: Peter F. Drucker and the Austrian School of Economics." *Management Decision.* 42, (10): 1269–1283.

Kirzner, Israel M. 1973. *Competition and Entrepreneurship.* Chicago: University of Chicago Press.

Kirzner, Israel M. 1979. *Perception, Opportunity and Profit: Studies in the Theory of Entrepreneurship.* Chicago and London: University of Chicago Press.

Kirzner, Israel M. 1985. *Discovery and the Capitalist Process.* Chicago: University of Chicago Press.

Kirzner, I. 1992. *The Meaning of Market Process.* London: Routledge.

Kirzner, Israel M. 1997. "Entrepreneurial Discovery and the Competitive Market Process: An Austrian Approach." *Journal of Economic Literature* 35: 60–85.

Klein, Peter G. 1996. "Economic Calculation and the Limits of Organization." *Review of Austrian Economics.* 9(2): 51–77.

Klein, Peter G. 2008. "Opportunity Discovery, Entrepreneurial Action, and Economic Organization." *Strategic Entrepreneurship Journal.* 2: 175–90.

Klein, Peter G. 2008a. "The Mundane Economics of the Austrian School." *Quarterly Journal of Austrian Economics.* 11(3–4): 165–87.

Klein, P.G. and Bylund, P.L. 2014. "The place of Austrian economics in contemporary entrepreneurship research." *Review of Austrian Economics.* 27(3): 259–279.

Klein, P.G. and S.R. Klein. 2001. "Do Entrepreneurs Make Predictable Mistakes? Evidence from Corporate Divestitures." *Quarterly Journal of Austrian Economics.* 4: 3–25.

Klein, Peter G., Anita M. McGahan, Joseph T. Mahoney, and Christos N. Pitelis. 2010. "Toward a Theory of Public Entrepreneurship." *European Management Review.* 7: 1–15.

Knight, Frank H. 1921. *Risk, Uncertainty, and Profit.* New York: August M. Kelley.

Knott, A.-M. 2003. Persistent Heterogeneity and Sustainable Innovation. *Strategic Management Journal.* 24: 687–705.

Lachmann, Ludwig M. 1956. *Capital and Its Structure.* Kansas City: Sheed Andrews and McMeel, 1978.

Lachmann, Ludwig M. 1969. "Methodological individualism and the market economy." *Roads to freedom: Essays in honour of Friedrich A. von Hayek* 89–103.

Lachmann, Ludwig M. 1977. *Capital, Expectations, and the Market Process.* Kansas City: Sheed Andrews and McMeel.

Langlois, Richard N. 2002. "Modularity in Technology and Organization." *Journal of Economic Behavior and Organization.* 49(1): 19–37.

Langlois, Richard N. 2003. "The Vanishing Hand: The Changing Dynamics of Industrial Capitalism." *Industrial and Corporate Change.* 12(2): 351–385.

Levinthal, Daniel. 1997. "Adaptation on Rugged Landscapes." *Management Science.* 43: 934–950.

Lewin, Peter and Steven E. Phelan. 2000. "An Austrian Theory of the Firm." *Review of Austrian Economics*. 13: 59–79.

Lippman, Steven A. and Richard P. Rumelt. 1982. "Uncertain Imitability: An Analysis of Interfirm Differences in Efficiency under Competition." *Bell Journal of Economics*. 13(2): 418–38.

Lippman, Steven A. and Rumelt, Richard P. 2003. "A Bargaining Perspective on Resource Advantage." *Strategic Management Journal*. 24: 1069–86.

Lucas, D.S. and Fuller, C.S. (2017). "Entrepreneurship: Productive, Unproductive, and Destructive—Relative to What? *Journal of Business Venturing Insights*. 7, 45–49.

Machaj,Mateusz. 2007. "Market Socialism and the Property Problem: Different Perspective of the Socialist Calculation Debate." *Quarterly Journal of Austrian Economics*. 10 (4): 257-280.

Mair, Johanna, and Ignasi Marti. 2006. "Social Entrepreneurship Research: A Source of Explanation, Prediction, and Delight." *Journal of World Business*. 41 (1): 36–44.

Martin, Dolores Tremewan. 1979. "Alternative Views of Mengerian Entrepreneurship." *History of Political Economy*. 11(2): 271–85.

Martin, Roger L., and Sally Osberg. 2007. "Social Enterprise: The Case for Definition." *Stanford Social Innovation Review*. 5 (2): 28–39.

Matsusaka, John G. 2001. "Corporate Diversification, Value Maximization, and Organizational Capabilities." *Journal of Business*. 74: 409–431.

Matthews, John. 2006. *Strategizing, Disequilibrium, and Profit*. Stanford: Stanford University Press.

Mathews, John. 2010. "Lachmannian insights into strategic entrepreneurship: Resources, activities and routines in a disequilibrium world." *Organization Studies*. 31(2): 219–44.

McCaffrey, M. 2009. "Entrepreneurship, Economic Evolution, and the End of Capitalism: Reconsidering Schumpeter's Thesis." *Quarterly Journal of Austrian Economics*. 12 (4), 3–21.

McCaffrey, M. 2013. Conflicting views of the entrepreneur in turn-of-the-century Vienna. *History of Economics Review*. 58(1), pp.27–43.

McCaffrey, M. 2014a. On the theory of entrepreneurial incentives and alertness. *Entrepreneurship Theory and Practice*. 38(4), pp.891–911.

McCaffrey, M. 2014b. "The Political Economy of the Art of War." *Comparative Strategy*. 33(4), 354–371.

McCaffrey, M. 2015a. "Economic Policy and Entrepreneurship: Alertness or Judgment?" In Bylund, P. Howden, D. (eds.) *The Next Generation of Austrian Economics: Essays in Honor of Joseph T. Salerno*. Auburn, Al: Ludwig von Mises Institute. pp.183–199.

McCaffrey, M. 2015b. "The Economics of Peace and War in the Chinese Military Classics." *Economics of Peace and Security Journal*. 10 (1): 23–31.

McCaffrey, M. 2016. Good Judgment, Good Luck: Frank Fetter's Neglected Theory of Entrepreneurship. *Review of Political Economy*. *28*(4), pp.504–522.

McCaffrey, M., 2017. "Military Strategy and Unproductive Entrepreneurship in Warring States China." *Management & Organizational History*, *12*(2), 99–118.

McCaffrey, M. 2018a. "Extending the Economic Foundations of Entrepreneurship Research." *European Management Review*. 15 (2): 191–199.

McCaffrey, M. 2018b. "William Baumol's "Entrepreneurship: Productive, Unproductive, and Destructive"." In *Foundational Research in Entrepreneurship Studies: Insightful* Contributions *and Future Pathways*, pp.179–201.

McCaffrey, M., & J.T. Salerno. 2011. "A Theory of Political Entrepreneurship." *Modern Economy*. 2 (4): 552–560.

McCaffrey, M., & J.T Salerno. 2014. Böhm-Bawerk's Approach to Entrepreneurship. *Journal of the History of Economic Thought*. *36*(4), pp.435–454.

Menger, Carl. [1871] 1985. *Principles of Economics*. New York: New York University Press.

Menger, C. 1883. *Untersuchungen über die Methode der Socialwissenschaften und der Politischen Oekonomie insbesondere*, Leipzig, Verlag von Duncker & Humblot. English translation by Francis J. Nock, Louis Schneider (ed.) 1963. Urbana: University of Illinois Press.

Milgrom, P. and J. Roberts. 1995. "Complementarities and Fit: Strategy, Structure, and Organizational Change in Manufacturing." *Journal of Accounting and Economics* 19: 179–208.

Mintzberg, H. 1990. "The Design School: Reconsidering the Basic Premises of Strategic Management." *Strategic Management Journal*. 11: 171–195

Mises, L. von. [1920] 1990. *Economic Calculation in the Socialist Commonwealth*. Auburn, Al: Ludwig von Mises Institute.

Mises,L. von. 1944, *Bureaucracy. New Haven*, CT: Yale University Press.

Mises, Ludwig von. 1949. *Human Action: A Treatise on Economics*. New Haven: Yale University Press.

Mises, Ludwig von. [1951] 2008, *Profit and Loss, Consumers-Producers Economic Services*. South Holland.

Montgomery, C.A. 1994. Corporate Diversification. *Journal of Economic Perspectives*, 8: 163–178.

Mort, G.S., Weerawardena, J., and K. Carnegie. 2003. "Social Entrepreneurship: Towards Conceptualisation." *International Journal of Nonprofit and Voluntary Sector Marketing*. 8 (1): 76–88.

Mosakowski, Elaine. 1997. "Strategy Making under Causal Ambiguity: Conceptual Issues and Empirical Evidence." *Organization Science.* 8:414–42.

Nelson, Richard R. and Sidney G. Winter. 1982. *An Evolutionary Theory of Economic Change.* Harvard: The Belknap Press.

Nell, Guinevere L. 2010. "Competition as Market Progress: An Austrian Rationale for Agent-Based Modeling." *Review of Austrian Economics.* 23 (2): 127–145.

Newman, J. 2018. "Contemporary Debates on Opportunity Cost Theory and Pedagogy." In Matthew McCaffrey, ed., *The Economic Theory of Costs: Foundations and New Directions.* Abingdon, UK: Routledge, pp. 11–26.

Nonaka,I., & Takeuchi, H. 1995. *The knowledge-creating company: How Japanese companies create the dynamics of innovation.* Oxford University Press.

Parker, S.C. 2004. *The Economics of Self-employment and Entrepreneurship.* Cambridge University Press.

Penrose, Edith T. 1959. *The Theory of the Growth of the Firm.* Oxford: Blackwell.

Peredo, A.M., and M. McLean. 2006. "Social Entrepreneurship: A Critical Review of the Concept." *Journal of World Business.* 41 (1): 56–65.

Peteraf, M. A. 1993. "The Cornerstones of Competitive Advantage: A Resource-Based view." *Strategic Management Journal.* 14: 179–91.

Peteraf, Margaret A. and Jay B. Barney. 2003. "Unraveling the Resource-Based Tangle." *Managerial and Decision Economics.* 24: 309–23.

Peters, T. 1994 *Liberation.* New York: Ballantine Books,

Porter, M.E. 1980. *Competitive strategy.* New York: Free Press.

Rajan, Raghuram G. and Julie Wulf. 2006. "The Flattening Firm: Evidence from Panel Data on the Changing Nature of Corporate Hierarchies." *Review of Economics and Statistics.* 88 (4): 759–773.

Rivkin, Jan W. 2000. "Imitation of Complex Strategies." *Management Science.* 46(6): 824–44.

Rothbard, Murray N. 1987. "Breaking Out of the Walrasian Box: The Cases of Schumpeter and Hansen." *Review of Austrian Economics.* 1 (1), 97–108.

Rothbard, Murray N. 1962. *Man, Economy, and State: A Treatise on Economic Principles.* 2_{nd} Scholar's Edition. Auburn, Al: Ludwig von Mises Institute, 2009.

Rothbard, M.N. 1985. "Professor Hébert on entrepreneurship." *Journal of Libertarian Studies.* 7(2): 281–286.

Rumelt, Richard P. 1982. "Diversification Strategy and Profitability." *Strategic Management Journal.* 3(4): 359–369.

Rumelt, Richard P. 1987. "Theory, Strategy, and Entrepreneurship." In David J. Teece, ed., *The Competitive Challenge.* San Francisco: Ballinger.

Salerno, Joseph T. 1990a. "Ludwig von Mises as Social Rationalist." *Review of Austrian Economics*. 4 (1): 26–54.

Salerno, Joseph T. 1990b. "Postscript: Why a Socialist Economy is 'Impossible'." In *Economic Calculation in the Socialist Commonwealth*. Auburn, AL: The Ludwig von Mises Institute.

Salerno, Joseph T. 1993. "Mises and Hayek Dehomogenized." *Review of Austrian Economics*. 6: 113–46.

Salerno, Joseph T. 2002. "The Rebirth of Austrian Economics—In Light of Austrian Economics." *Quarterly Journal of Austrian Economics*. 5(4): 111–128.

Salerno, J.T. 2008. The entrepreneur: real and imagined. *Quarterly Journal of Austrian Economics*. 11(3-4): 188-207.

Sarasvathy, Saras D. 2008. *Effectuation: Elements of Entrepreneurial Expertise*, Northampton: Edward Elgar Publishing.

Schultz, Theodore W. 1980. "Investment in Entrepreneurial Ability." *Scandinavian Journal of Economics*. 82(4): 437–448.

Schumpeter, J.A., 1908. *Das Wesen und der Hauptinhalt der theoretischen Nationalökonomie*. Duncker & Humbolt.

Schumpeter, Joseph A. 1934. *The Theory of Economic Development*. Cambridge, Mass.: Harvard University Press.

Seelos, Christian, and Johanna Mair. 2005. "Social Entrepreneurship: Creating New Business Models to Serve the Poor." *Business Horizons*. 48 (3): 241–246.

Shackle, George L.S. 1972. *Epistemics and Economics*. Cambridge: Cambridge University Press.

Shane, Scott. 2000. "Prior Knowledge and the Discovery of Entrepreneurial Opportunities." *Organization Science*. 11: 448–469.

Shane, Scott. 2003. *A General Theory of Entrepreneurship*. Cheltenham: Edward Elgar.

Shane, Scott. and S. Venkataraman. 2000. "The Promise of Entrepreneurship as a Field of Research." *Academy of Management Review*. 25: 217–226.

Shaver, Kelly G., and Linda R. Scott. 1991. "Person, Process, Choice: The Psychology of New Venture Creation." *Entrepreneurship Theory and Practice*. 16: 23–45.

Shepherd, D., 2015, "Party on! A Call for Entrepreneurship Research that is More Interactive, Activity Based, Cognitively Hot, Compassionate, and Prosocial." *Journal of Business Venturing*. 30: 489–507.

Siggelkow, Nicolai and Daniel A. Levinthal. 2003. "Temporarily Divide to Conquer: Centralized, Decentralized, and Reintegrated Organizational

Approaches to Exploration and Adaptation." *Organization Science*. 14(6): 650–669.

Simon, Herbert A. 1951. "A Formal Theory of the Employment Relationship." *Econometrica* 293–305.

Simon, Herbert A. 1962. "The Architecture of Complexity." *Proceedings of the American Philosophical Society* 106(6): 467–482.

Spitznagel, Mark. 2013. *The Dao of Capital*. Hoboken, NJ: Wiley.

Staubus, George J. 1986. "The Market Simulation Theory of Accounting Measurement." *Accounting and Business Research*. 16: 117–132.

Stern, J. M., Stewart, G. B. and Chew, D. H. 1995. "The EVA Financial Management System." *Journal of Applied Corporate Finance*. 8: 32–46.

Tapscott, D. and A.D. Williams, 2008. *Wikinomics: How Mass Collaboration Changes Everything*. New York: Portfolio Trade.

Taylor, Thomas C. 2000. "Current Developments in Cost Accounting and the Dynamics of Economic Calculation." *Quarterly Journal of Austrian Economics*. 3(2): 3–19.

Teece, David J. 1986. "Profiting from Technological Innovation. *Research Policy*. 15: 285–305.

Teece, David J. 2009. *Dynamic capabilities and strategic management: Organizing for innovation and growth*. Oxford University Press.

Topan, Mihai Vladimir. 2012. "A Note on Rothbardian Decision-Making Rents." *Quarterly Journal of Austrian Economics*. 15(1): 75–88.

Vaughn, Karen I. 1994. *Austrian Economics in America*. Cambridge: Cambridge University Press.

Waldman, Don. and Elizabeth Jensen. 2016. *Industrial organization: theory and practice*. Routledge.

Wernerfelt, Birger. 1984. "A Resource-Based View of the Firm." *Strategic Management Journal*. 5: 272–80.

Wieser, Friedrich A. von. 1914. *Social Economics*. London: Oxford University Press, 1928.

Williamson, Oliver E. 1975. *Markets and Hierarchies: Analysis and Antitrust Implications*. New York: Free Press.

Williamson, Oliver E. 1985. *The Economic Institutions of Capitalism*. New York: Free Press.

Williamson, O.E. 1991. Economic Institutions: Spontaneous and Intentional Governance. *Journal of Law, Economics, and Organization*. 7: 159–187.

Williamson OE. 2000. The new institutional economics: taking stock, looking ahead. *Journal of Economic Literature* 38, 595–613.

Young, G., Smith, K.G., and Grimm, C.M. 1996. "Austrian" and Industrial Organization Perspectives on Firm-Level Competitive Activity and Performance. *Organization Science.* 7: 243-254.

Zahra, S. A., Gedajlovic, E., Neubaum, D. O., & Shulman, J. M. 2009. "A Typology of Social Entrepreneurs: Motives, Search Processes and Ethical Challenges." *Journal of Business Venturing.* 24(5): 519–32.

Cambridge Elements $\equiv$

Business Strategy

J.-C. Spender
Rutgers Business School

J.-C. Spender is a visiting scholar at Rutgers Business School and a research Professor, Kozminski University. He has been active in the business strategy field since 1971 and is the author or co-author of seven books and numerous papers. His principal academic interest is in knowledge-based theories of the private sector firm, and managing them.

About the Series

Business strategy's reach is vast, and important too since wherever there is business activity there is strategizing. As a field, strategy has a long history from medieval and colonial times to today's developed and developing economies. This series offers a place for interesting and illuminating research including industry and corporate studies, strategizing in service industries, the arts, the public sector, and the new forms of internet-based commerce. It also covers today's expanding gamut of analytic techniques.

Cambridge Elements ≡

Business Strategy

CPSIA information can be obtained
at www.ICGtesting.com
Printed in the USA
LVHW031922211019
634872LV00014B/442/P

9 781108 745802